OKINAWA
1945

OKINAWA
1945

DR. T. M. HUBER

COMPENDIUM

First published 2003

ISBN 1 902579 73 9

© Compendium Publishing, 2003

Printed and bound in China through Printworks Int. Ltd.

Published by Compendium, 43 Frith Street, Soho, London, W1D 4SA

Editor's note

Throughout the book names of Japanese personalities are shown in the order family name then given name, thus Colonel Yahara appears in full as Yahara Hiromichi

Publishing History

Japan's Battle of Okinawa April–June 1945 was first published by the Combat Studies Institute in 1990. It was then published, with additions, by The Military Press in 2001. This book is the Military Press edition redesigned with new artwork and photographs.

Acknowledgements

Photo research by John D. Gresham, ably assisted by Melissa K. Day. The photographs in this book are Official U.S. Navy photographs except for the following:

Official U.S. Marine Corps: 74, 78, 79, 101 (below), 111, 128, 129, 132.

Office of War Information: 10, 11, 20, 22, 23, 27, 28, 29, 48, 49 (top), 50, 62 (both), 66 (below), 67, 68, 69, 70, 73, 75, 80, 84, 88 (inset), 94, 100 (below), 101 (above), 112 (left), 140, 144, 160.

Official U.S. Army Signal Corps: 17, 46 (below), 60 (below), 61 (below), 63, 66 (above), 97, 99, 102, 110, 152.

Atomic Energy Commission: 146

Cover: *Battleship USS* Tennessee *(BB-43) bombards Okinawa just before H-Hour on 1st April, part of the heaviest naval bombardment of the war in support of a landing – 44,825 rounds of gunfire, 32,000 rockets and 22,500 mortar shells pounded the Japanese before the Amtracs went in.*

Previous page: *Japanese kamikaze aircraft crashes into sea alongside USS* Essex *(CV-9).*

Below: *Okinawa and surrounding islands.*

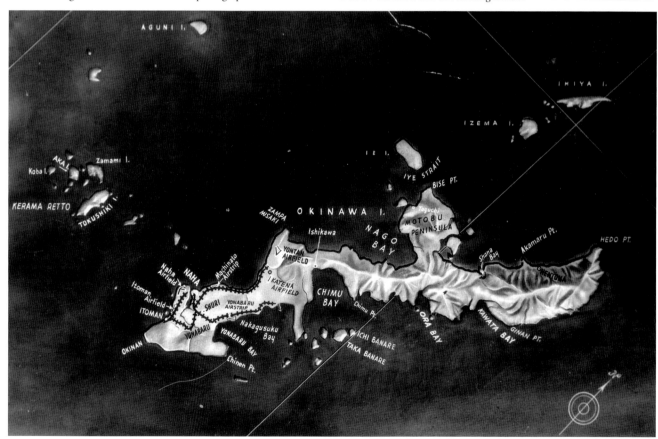

Contents

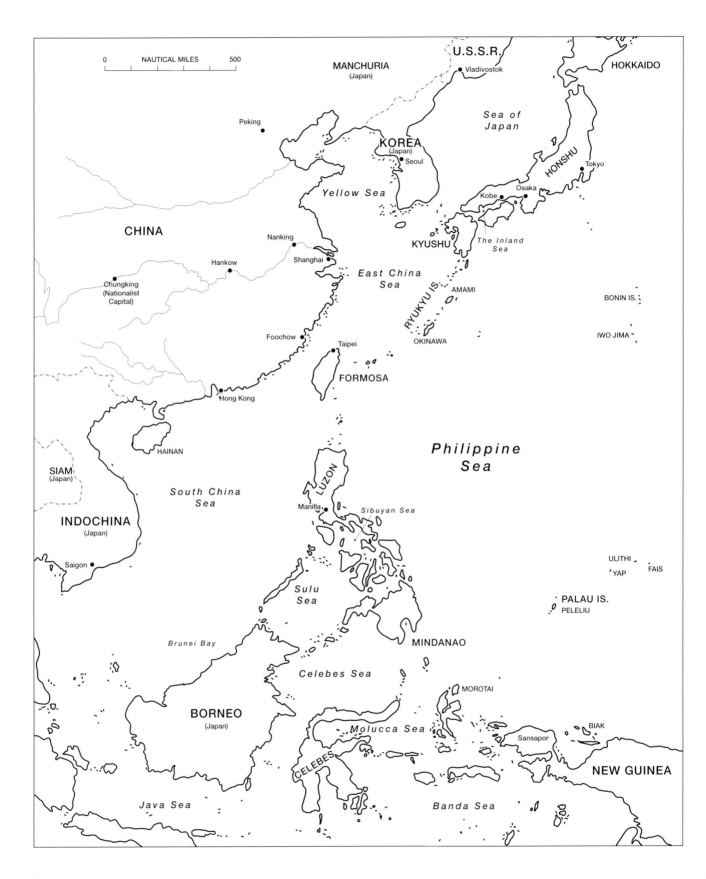

MANCHURIA
(Japan)

U.S.S.R.

HOKKAIDO

Vladivostok

Peking

Sea of
Japan

KOREA
(Japan)

Seoul

HONSHU

Tokyo

Yellow Sea

Osaka

Kobe

CHINA

Nanking

KYUSHU

The Inland
Sea

Hankow

Shanghai

East China
Sea

Chungking
(Nationalist
Capital)

RYUKYU IS.

AMAMI

BONIN IS.

Foochow

Taipei

OKINAWA

IWO JIMA

FORMOSA

Hong Kong

HAINAN

LUZON

Philippine
Sea

SIAM
(Japan)

South China
Sea

Manilla

Sibuyan Sea

ULITHI

FAIS

YAP

INDOCHINA
(Japan)

PALAU IS.

PELELIU

Saigon

Sulu
Sea

Brunei Bay

MINDANAO

Celebes Sea

MOROTAI

BORNEO
(Japan)

Molucca Sea

BIAK

Sansapor

CELEBES

NEW GUINEA

Java Sea

Banda Sea

NAUTICAL MILES

0

500

Preface

Introduction

During the Pacific War, from 1937 to 1945, the Japanese military grew to an end strength of 7 million men. Over the course of the war this represented some 28 million man-years of uniformed service to the Japanese Empire. Imperial service spanned every conceivable environment, from sub-arctic conditions in Manchuria to steaming rain forest in New Guinea, and every conceivable adversary, from a Soviet armoured corps at Nomonhan in 1939 to isolated nationalist guerrillas in the Philippine archipelago. Moreover, there is abundant literature in Japanese on these experiences in the form of official histories, unit histories, memoirs, biographies, and studies by scholars and journalists. There is a rich harvest of military lessons that can be reaped from these extensive resources. Even so, this material has been left largely untouched by US military theorists in the past because of the obstacle presented by the Japanese language.

T. M. Huber

The Okinawa Campaign of April–June 1945 was the last major operation undertaken by United States' forces prior to the planned invasion of Japan. This account is based principally on Japanese sources and written from the Japanese viewpoint. This history has not, until now, been generally available, despite the fact that since its original publication, it has been often been referred to in other histories of World War II in the Pacific.

This edition has three additional chapters 6, 7, and 8; also the maps have been redrawn and printed in colour. Chapter 6 is a study of the role of US Army Engineers during the campaign. Engineer units played a vital role in the suppression and destruction of the system of defences the Japanese had constructed. Chapter 7 is a brief examination of the problems facing an invasion of Japan in the light of those difficulties that were met by American forces in the Okinawa Campaign. From recent studies that have been based on the examination of contemporary records it would seem that the invasion would in all probability not have taken place. Chapter 8 presents the reports which resulted from the interrogations, on Okinawa, of Colonel Yahara and Mr Sita. Colonel Yahara was the operations officer of the 32nd Army and Mr Sita was the secretary of Lt-General Cho, chief of staff of the 32nd Army.

Lowry Cole
Editor

Left: *The seat of war – Okinawa is to the southwest of Kyushu.*

Chapter 1 Anticipation of the Battle, March 1944 – March 1945

The Battle of Okinawa, 1st April to 22nd June 1945, is known to English language readers through a variety of accounts, both official and commercial publications. Some of these works focus on operations, and some provide personal perspectives, so that most major features of the American experience on Okinawa are well understood. However, another whole dimension of the Okinawa struggle is not as well known: Japan's Okinawa. To staff and front-line soldiers of the Imperial Japanese Army (IJA), the events of Okinawa appeared quite differently than they did to their American counterparts. For the Japanese, the operational problems were different, the solutions were different, and the perceived results from day to day were different. American combat experiences on Okinawa teach us something about the lethality of modern warfare; Japanese experiences on Okinawa may teach us still more.

The Japanese Empire's strategic need to hold Okinawa was absolute. After US air strikes on Truk in February 1944, Imperial General Headquarters (IGHQ) assumed that the United States sooner or later would try to seize Okinawa as an advanced base for invading Japan itself and accordingly garrisoned the island with the newly organised 32nd Army. As time went by, it became apparent that any US assault on Okinawa would enjoy air and artillery superiority, abundant naval artillery

Below: Truk Harbor following the attack by US carrier-based planes on 16th February 1944.

cover, superior firepower on the battlefield, and predominance in armour. Japan's 32nd Army knew well in advance both where it would fight on Okinawa and that it would face certain destruction.

Although the large Japanese garrison on Okinawa was as well supplied as it could be with men, provisions, and artillery, it was not well prepared at first with doctrine and training. When Japan's Greater East Asia War began in 1937, its army was conceived as, and was, a superior infantry force. It relied on infiltration, manoeuvre, bold attack, and close combat tactics to prevail over its adversaries, the Chinese and European colonial garrisons. Beginning with Guadalcanal, however, Japan faced an adversary with more firepower than itself on a confined island terrain. For an isolated Japanese island garrison subject to devastating offshore bombardment, manoeuvre and close combat skills were of little use. In fact, the IJA's received operational methods were completely inappropriate to the re-alities of most battles of the Pacific campaign, including Okinawa.

The latest trends in strategic doctrine being developed by IGHQ were also completely unsuitable as it turned out. IGHQ expected the defence of Okinawa to be achieved mainly by air power and envisioned Okinawa as a gigantic air base. In the eyes of IGHQ, 32nd Army's mission was only to build the airstrips, then to provide service support for the air operations and security on the ground for the fields. In fact, however, severe

Above: Truk was Japan's main naval base in the Central Pacific. At the left is Dublon Island; center foreground is Eten Island, a large air base. Note two aircraft carriers lying at anchor at center right.

Below: Japanese cruiser burning and listing during the attack. Note torpedo wake approaching ship from the right upper center of picture.

shortages of planes and pilots made air defence of Okinawa unfeasible. The IJA's long-standing infantry doctrine prescribed too little equipment for the 32nd Army, at the same time as the new high technology air strategy required far more state-of-the-

art equipment than existed. The 32nd Army was stranded between the two incompatible concepts.

How, then, did Japan's 32nd Army cope with the problem of overwhelming enemy fire power and its own doctrine's total inadequacy? The 32nd Army staff became locked in controversy over these problems, but in the end, ignoring their tradition and their superiors, they resolved to dig deep, contest the ground foot by foot, and use bold counter-attack only selectively as an instrument of defence. Ultimately their methods resembled the fluid defence-in-depth tactics developed by German forces in World War I, though these methods would be used effectively here to oppose modern tanks and aircraft.

Early Preparations – The Air Strategy

For the Americans the Okinawa campaign began on 1st April 1945, the day US forces landed (L-Day). For the Japanese high command, however, the defence of Okinawa began over a year before. American air strikes against Truk in February 1944 made it clear to Japanese strategists that the Marianas line could fall, leaving the Ryukyu line as the main zone of defence. There then began a year of operational analysis, political manoeuvring, re-organisation, the development of the facilities, and the build-up of supplies that would determine as much as anything else the performance of Japanese forces on Okinawa. Japanese commentators sometimes even leave the impression that these preparations were all important for the outcome and that the events that took place during the fighting were of minor consequence. Surviving staff officers were convinced that decisions made the year before L-Day critically affected what happened.

It was one of the peculiarities of the Okinawa campaign that the defenders knew well in advance of the American attack exactly where the battle was likely to be fought, and therefore the type of terrain that would have to be defended. Okinawa Island is only 2–18 miles wide and 60 miles long, a small place for a violent clash of major powers, compared to, say, North Africa or the open Pacific. This battle area ensured that the fighting would be intense, involving densely packed forces supported by overwhelming firepower. These obvious facts conditioned the Japanese response.

In February 1944, just after the Truk air raids, IGHQ's 'Outline of Preparations for the TEI-Go Operation' provided for an increased defence presence in the area of the Ryukyu Islands and Taiwan. To this end IGHQ created the 32nd Army headquarters late in March, to be located at Naha, Okinawa. Its first commander, Lieutenant-General Watanabe Masao, assumed his post on 1st April 1944, a year to the day before the Okinawa landings.

The Ryukyus and Taiwan were to form a long group of interlocking air bases under the TEI-Go scheme as well as in the later plans that were developed. These bases were expected to defeat any American sea or air forces sent into the region. To avoid destruction from the air, each base was to consist of a cluster of airfields, so that if one were damaged others could be used immediately. Military and civilian construction teams were promptly set to work building the numerous fields. Thirteen base clusters had to be created, stretching in a line from Tachiarai in the northern Ryukyus to Pingting on Taiwan in the south. IGHQ's extravagant scheme for this invulnerable air wall derived from its recent experiences on New Guinea. Japan's 4th Air Army there had no success destroying the Allied air base at Port Moresby because it consisted of six adjoining runways, protected by a dense radar and air defence organisation. IGHQ concluded that this same style of aviation fortress could effectively guard the Ryukyu line against naval approaches.

Above: *US Marines examine the bodies of Japanese soldiers at Guadalcanal in the Solomons. The battle for Guadalcanal took six months of bloody fighting in 1942 but by the end of it, the US held the initiative in the Pacific War.*

Left: *Dead Japanese and a Type 94 tankette on Saipan in the Marianas. Assaulted in June 1944, Saipan's fall in early July gave US B-29s the base they needed to bomb mainland Japan.*

The only remaining tasks for ground forces were the defence of these facilities and their maritime anchorages through which the supplies were shipped – once the unenviable work of building the fields themselves was complete. Much of the energy of 32nd Army would be absorbed, almost up to L-Day, building these air facilities. This was the more difficult since 32nd Army had only two bulldozers and one earth roller. Japan had produced bulldozers in small numbers at its Komatsu plant since 1943, but few had reached the front. Since soldiers were thus obliged to use shovels, hoes, straw baskets, and horse-drawn wagons, construction was slow. Moreover, because of the US submarine campaign, it was impossible for the Japanese to deliver the large quantities of fuel, ammunition, and anti-aircraft guns needed to operate the bases. Even more seriously, the planes themselves were not available.

Above: The first wave of marines to hit the beach on Saipan did so under heavy Japanese fire. Casualties in the month-long battle for the island were high: the Japanese lost some 30,000; US dead numbered 3,426 with 10,500 wounded.

Above right: Mount Suribachi on Iwo Jima. The battle for Iwo Jima lasted from 19th February 1945 to the end of May. US casualties were 30% of the landing forces: 6,812 killed and 19,189 wounded.

Far right: IJA 32nd Army positions on Okinawa, August–November 1944.

Below: A cigarette break on Peleliu. Two months' fighting cost the US forces 1,792 killed and 8,011 wounded – a 40% casualty rate.

In May 1944, 32nd Army had only enough forces to protect facilities on the island from minor raids. The 32nd Army staff expected that American forces might assault Okinawa at the same time as a thrust into the Marianas or alternatively might attack the Marianas first and not Okinawa until the spring of 1945. This meant that the 32nd Army's staff from the beginning lived with the foreboding of an immediate assault.

As a result of the loss of Saipan in July 1944 IGHQ's TEI-Go plans were superseded in that month by the SHO-Go plans. The several SHO-Go plans covered each area from northern Japan to the Philippines. The Philippines were covered by SHO-Go One and the Ryukyu area by SHO-Go Two. The plans called for 1,500 planes to converge from China, Taiwan, and the Philippines should US forces enter the Ryukyu area.

At the same time, noting the loss of Saipan, IGHQ began rushing major ground forces to Okinawa. The 15th Independent Mixed Regiment was sent immediately by air in July 1944. (The 15th would later be absorbed by the 44th Independent Mixed Brigade [IMB].) The other major units that were sent to Okinawa in July and August were the 24th Division, the 62nd Division, the 9th Division, and the 44th IMB, all infantry formations. Infantry units were also sent to Miyako, Ishigaki, Tokuno, Daito, and other neighbouring islands.

The premiss at this time was that most US forces would be destroyed at sea and that Japanese resources would be abundant. Therefore, 32nd Army's strategy was to occupy all of Okinawa in force and to destroy the invasion party on whichever beach it

appeared (see map 1). The 44th IMB was positioned on Motobu Peninsula and Ie Island. The 24th Division was on the plain facing the Hagushi beaches. The 62nd Division was on the narrow neck of land north of Urasoe-Mura, and the 9th Division in the area south of Urasoe-Mura. If the Americans landed at Itoman, the 24th and 62nd Divisions were to move south. If they landed at Hagushi, the 9th and 62nd Divisions were to move north. The tendency of 32nd Army staff after the autumn of 1944, however, would be increasingly to concentrate these forces until almost all were deployed south of Uchitomari and their operational plans became increasingly defensive.

The rapid build up of ground forces in July and August 1944 occurred because IGHQ felt Okinawa might be a target immediately after Saipan. But with American landings on Palau and Leyte in September and October, IGHQ realised that the Philippines, not Okinawa, was the Americans' next objective. The fierce fighting on Leyte, under the rubric of SHO-Go One, affected 32nd Army in several ways. Rigorous training of troops began, including divisional manoeuvres to every conceivable American landing point. Night attacks on bridges were practised. Staffs at all levels studied positions and strategy. At the end of October artillery units practised bombarding beachheads with live shells, a demonstration that reassured the prefectural governor and civilian observers more than it did the 32nd Army staff. Even so, the rigorous training served to restore the troops' and officers' confidence, which had wavered in the face of the early news from Leyte.

Unfortunately, it was at this time that IGHQ chose to withdraw the elite 9th Division from Okinawa to participate in the Leyte battle. On 13 November 1944, 32nd Army staff members received a telegram from IGHQ instructing them to designate their best division, which staff members agreed was the 9th, for redeployment to the Philippines. The staff vigorously protested this removal of the 9th Division at the staff meeting in Taipei where it was discussed in early November, and continued to protest it right up to L-Day. Survivors still protest about this decision. The 32nd Army staff's resentment over this was the greater since the 9th Division was actually sent to Taiwan, not to the Philippines, Taiwan being another possible target of American landings and a competitor with Okinawa for scarce resources. The fact that Taiwan's 10th Area Army headquarters was superior to the 32nd Army in the chain of command, and may have selfishly engineered the move, made these feelings of resentment all the greater.

The unexpected removal of the organisation's best division threw 32nd Army's operational plans into turmoil. Ironically it had a highly advantageous effect on fighting efficiency. It forced 32nd Army to do more with less, to economise, something IJA staffs had rarely done in the past. Removal of the 9th Division must have shaken 32nd Army staff members into realizing that they alone were the masters of events on Okinawa; IGHQ had other interests to pursue.

Withdrawal of the 9th Division was the crisis for the 32nd Army staff that forced them into a comprehensive review not only of their operational plans but of their operational doctrine. The upshot of this crisis was a set of options, presented on 23rd November 1944 by the senior operations officer, Colonel Yahara Hiromichi, to 32nd Army's chief of staff, Lieutenant-General Cho Isamu. Yahara's options of 23rd November represented just four

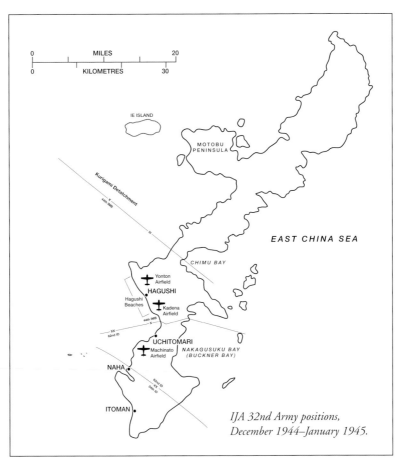

IJA 32nd Army positions, December 1944–January 1945.

These four respective options corresponded, roughly speaking, to Japanese methods on:

(1) Guadalcanal, where contact with the main American force was piecemeal.

(2) Saipan, where suicidal attack in the open brought early defeat.

(3) Iwo Jima, which was still to take place, where there would be a dogged dug-in defence near airfields the Americans needed.

(4) Luzon, also still to take place, where Japanese forces would withdraw to the northern mountains and survive to the end of the war intact but strategically passive.

possible dispositions of 32nd Army's finite resources on Okinawa, but each of the four positions required a completely different operational doctrine! Yahara's four schemes covered every major method the Japanese would use in the Pacific fighting. Yahara's four approaches were, in brief:

(1) After the 9th Division's removal, available forces should be spread thinly to defend all of Okinawa.

(2) Forces should be deployed only in the Nakagami area, on the level plains opposite the potential Hagushi landing beaches and where the Yontan and Kadena airfields were positioned.

(3) Forces should be deployed only in the mountainous and easily defensible Shimajiri area, which is the southern area where the Japanese could still control the port of Naha and interdict the northern airfields with artillery

(4) Forces should be deployed in the Kunigami area, namely the mountainous areas in the far north that were easily defensible and did not invite attack because they had no strategic value.

To sum up, 32nd Army could attempt to defend all of Okinawa or only the centre, only the south, or only the north.

Yahara's memorandum of 23rd November 1944 rejected the first option, defence of all Okinawa, as no longer feasible due to the lack of forces, even though IGHQ favoured it. He rejected the second option, defence of the open Hagushi plain, even though it might briefly protect the IGHQ's treasured airfields, because by doing so 32nd Army would be immediately annihilated. He rejected the fourth option, cowering in the northern hills, even though it would keep the army unharmed, because in strategic terms, it would totally waste the resources over which the 32nd Army staff was the steward.

Instead, Yahara endorsed the third option, concentrating all forces in the defensible but strategically critical south. Chief of staff Cho agreed and passed the proposal to the 32nd Army commander, Lieutenant-General Ushijima Mitsuru, who adopted it without comment as 32nd Army policy. Although this change in deployment seemed workaday, it actually entailed a massive and controversial change in 32nd Army's operational doctrine. It meant abandoning the IJA's heretofore cherished policy of 'decisive battle', namely seeking out the enemy aggressively in close combat, in favour of a 'war of attrition'. It meant deliberately discarding the priority of anti-naval air defence that for ten months had been, and still would be, the cornerstone of IGHQ's Pacific strategy. The 32nd Army staff's new commitment to attrition warfare in the south of the island was probably more important than any other event in making the IJA's performance on Okinawa, along with that on Iwo Jima, the most militarily effective of the Pacific War. The 32nd Army staff members were pleased with the new arrangement as a solid plan that would allow them to give a good account of themselves, and it was sent to the units on 26 November.

The new plan

Above: General Douglas MacArthur, Allied Supreme Commander in the Southwest Pacific, observing the landings on Leyte from the bridge of USS Nashville.

the Americans landed at Hagushi and to join the 24th Division if the Americans landed near Itoman. Similarly, the 24th Division was expected to help defend against landings north of Itoman and to join the 62nd Division if there was fighting on the Machinato beaches or to the north. In other words, the Americans were to be met with a solid front if they landed anywhere on the rugged isthmus or on the southern area, but they were not to be engaged heavily if they landed on the open Hagushi plain. Moreover, in case of an attack at Itoman or Machinato, the Americans were to be fired on from the nearby mountains, then

contained five paragraphs. The 44th IMB was stationed on the Hagushi plain, the 62nd Division was placed on the central isthmus, and the 24th Division was deployed on the southern end of the island (see map 2). The Kunigami Detachment was the only unit north of the Hagushi plain and on the Motobu Peninsula. The enemy 'was to be contained by a strategic delaying action', not openly attacked for a 'decisive battle'. To placate IGHQ, the 44th IMB was placed in positions covering the Yontan and Kadena airfields. It was supposed to protect the fields as long as possible if the Americans landed at Hagushi and to counter-attack if the occasion offered. In reality, however, the 32nd Army staff intended for 44th IMB merely to harass the Americans and fall back southward toward the 62nd Division's lines. The 32nd Army staff also expected 44th IMB to prevent early seizure of the airfields by American airborne troops.

The 62nd Division, on the central isthmus, was to repel possible American landings on the beaches near the Machinato airfield. It was also to prepare to fight on a line facing north if

driven off the beaches in a 'decisive battle'. This was believed reasonably possible because the mountains extended near to the shore, offering good defensive protection and also denying to the landing force the room it needed for staging.

In December 1944 the commander of 10th Area Army on Taiwan, General Rikichi, summoned 32nd Army chief of staff Cho to Taipei to justify the new dispositions. Ando favoured annihilating the Americans on the beaches as earlier doctrine required. He acquiesced in the new November dispositions, however, perhaps because he knew the 32nd Army staff was still resentful over the recent loss of the 9th Division, which was what had necessitated the redeployment in November.

The new force dispositions were carried out in December, and the new lines were inspected by operations officer Yahara in January. Yahara's prevalent impression, however, was that the defences were too thin to hold against concentrated attack. IJA doctrine required no more than six miles of front per division. The 32nd Army's two and a half divisions were covering 36 miles of front, of which 24 miles had to be actively defended. Yahara concluded that the division fronts would have to be shortened, and that the way to do this was to move 44th IMB from the Hagushi plain to the south to take over some of the area covered by the 62nd Division (see map 3). The new arrangement was endorsed by Cho and Ushijima and sent to the divisional units on 15th January 1945.

The dispositions of 15th January would endure until the American landings on 1st April. They represented a culmination of the tendency of the 32nd Army staff, facing the prospect of American firepower, to shorten its lines and give up its offensive plans. In the end 32nd Army only defended the southernmost area of the

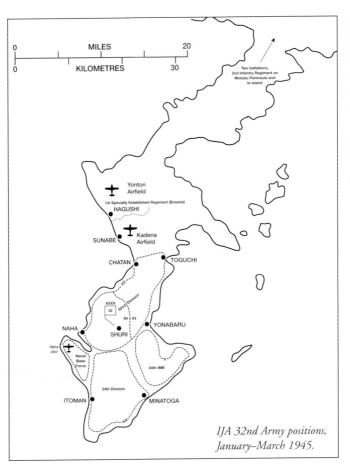

IJA 32nd Army positions, January–March 1945.

Army staff received a second signal saying the dispatch of the 84th Division had been rescinded. Lieutenant-General Miyazaki, head of the strategy branch of the IGHQ, claimed that he agonised over the decision but was ultimately reluctant to send forces from the Home Islands when Japan itself might soon be under attack. Reasonable as this was, the decision did nothing for the morale of the forces on Okinawa and merely confirmed their conviction that IGHQ was not going to send them the resources they needed.

The staff officers on Okinawa felt that their headquarters had abandoned them and that, eventually, they would be overwhelmed and destroyed by the Americans. They expected

island and abandoned the Yontan and Kadena airfields uncontested. In the eyes of IGHQ, Okinawa was part of a multi-theatre, technology-intensive strategy in which 32nd Army's specialised role was to defend the Yontan and Kadena airfields. The 32nd Army staff members' perceptions were simpler: 32nd Army was about to be attacked and needed defensible positions to survive. The staff members had no confidence that air forces could halt the Americans and instead thought simply in terms of denying the Americans free use of Okinawa facilities as long as possible. Their larger strategic assumptions were well informed and in fact were more sound than the air power schemes of IGHQ. Even so, the staff's final operational plans amounted to nothing more nor less than denying the enemy the ground, foot by foot.

On 23rd January 1944, 32nd Army received a signal from IGHQ saying that the 84th Division in Himeji would be sent to Okinawa to replace the 9th Division, which had been transferred to Taiwan. IGHQ had promised to provide a replacement in November of the previous year when the 9th Division was withdrawn. That same evening, however, the 32nd

the Americans to land between six and ten divisions against the Japanese garrison which now consisted of two and a half divisions. The staff calculated that superior quality and numbers of weapons gave each US division five or six times the firepower of a Japanese division. This meant that US firepower on the ground would be at least twelve times Japanese firepower. To this would be added the Americans' abundant naval and air firepower. Understandably, January 1945 was a time of dark thoughts and sullen inactivity for the 32nd Army staff.

To alleviate this mood, Colonel Yahara prepared a pamphlet titled *The Road to Certain Victory* in which he argued that, through the use of fortifications, 32nd Army could defeat the Americans' superior numbers and technology. Building and using tunnels, what he called 'sleeping tactics', was the method he recommended as suitable and likely to bring success. Lt-Gen Cho deleted the few lines that were pessimistic and then had the pamphlet printed and distributed. The pamphlet's purpose was to get the troops and officers stimulated to work on their fortifications, which they did in a mood of renewed optimism.

Work on the caves now began with great vigour. 'Confidence in victory will be born from strong fortifications' was the soldiers' slogan. The caves meant shelter for the soldiers from the fierce bombardments that were sure to come, and they also offered a gleam of hope of victory. The combination was irresistible, and units began to work enthusiastically on their own caves. Moreover, after frequent movements, the units were finally in the positions where they would remain until the Americans landed. The 62nd Division and the 24th Division would be in their final positions 100 days and the 44th IMB 50 days before L-Day.

Enthusiasm was essential because of the great exertion it took to create the caves. Just as 32nd Army had only two bulldozers to build the airfields, it had no mechanised tunnelling equipment at all.

Above: *Field Marshal Hajime Sugiyama of Japan, Minister of War in the Kuniaki Koiso cabinet, who was tasked in April 1945 with the job of defending eastern Japan and Operation 'Ketsu-Go' – the expulsion of enemy forces before they could achieve a bridgehead on the Japanese homeland.*

Cho repeatedly requested such equipment, so often, in fact, that 'Cho's rock-cutters' became famous in the corridors of IGHQ. Still, none were sent. In lieu of cutting machines, the soldiers could only use their entrenching tools and shovels.

Besides lacking cutting equipment, 32nd Army lacked construction materials. It had no cement, no iron reinforcement, and no dynamite. The units had to rely entirely on wooden beams that they obtained themselves to shore up their shafts. This was not easy because there were no forests in the south of the island where the troops were now positioned. Pine forests were abundant in the mountainous north, however, so each unit was assigned its own area in the north to gather the timber it needed. Several hundred men from each division were detailed for this work. The problem remained, however, of how to move the several million logs that were needed over the 40 or so miles from the forests to the excavations. There was no railway, and although 32nd Army had trucks, the 10th October air raids on

Naha had destroyed most of the fuel they needed. The trucks, therefore, could not be used for the work of moving the logs. The solution was for each unit to cut its own logs, then transport them in small native boats called sabenis. The divisions acquired 70 of these, which then plied the waters steadily from north to south. In January 1945, however, the Leyte-based B-24s that began flying over daily for reconnaissance also began strafing the boats. So the waterborne delivery of logs had to be switched from day to night, greatly lowering efficiency.

Other problems cave builders found had to do with the quality of the soil. Local geological conditions made it possible for the finished tunnel positions to be highly resistant to fire, although these same conditions made building the tunnels difficult. The whole island south of Futema consisted of coral stone that was 30–60 feet thick and as hard as concrete. This was not the case in the north, which was one of the reasons Yahara had abandoned the north in November. Digging through the coral took tremendous effort, and soldiers wore their picks and entrenching tools to stumps. Once through the coral crust, however, the earth was a soft red clay, relatively easy to excavate. In addition, there were natural caves in each area of the south that soldiers could take over and develop. Some of these natural caves could accommodate 1,000 men each. Soldiers felt the thick coral crust was as good as a ferro-concrete roof for their caves, and indeed the caves would protect their inhabitants from bombing and shell fire.

The 32nd Army intended to, and did, move its entire force underground. The caves were made large enough to hold all personnel, weapons, ammunition, provisions, and 'all other material'. Prior to November 1944 each unit had been expected to build caves for three times its own numbers so that troops

Above and Above right: *The main portion of the native Okinawans were moved to Japan; others were pressed into service as soldiers or labourers, with some 39,000 drafted. Once the US forces arrived on the island, many Okinawans were placed in internment camps such as the one at Sobe shown here.*

from other areas could be concentrated in any area and remain underground. This more ambitious goal had to be abandoned in November 1944, however, when the major troop movements reduced the number of working days in each unit's new sector. Still, 32nd Army built 60 miles of underground fortifications.

The 32nd Army devised elaborate anti-tank construction schemes. A system of anti-tank trenches was to be built. In addition there were to be foxholes on likely tank routes and anti-tank minefields, as well as the blocking and destruction of major tank routes. The projected anti-tank trench system was especially ambitious. Almost no progress was made building it, however, because 32nd Army was obliged to devote what time was left to the construction of the IGHQ's airfields.

The 32nd Army strove to strengthen its fighting personnel as well as its fortifications. It evacuated a portion of Okinawa's population of 435,000 to the main Japanese islands, partly for their safety and partly to prevent their consuming precious foodstuffs once communications with the outside were cut off. Some 80,000 Okinawans were moved to Kyushu on munitions vessels that would otherwise return to Japan empty. Because the shipping space was scarce and the inhabitants reluctant to leave, the Army also began moving Okinawans from the populous southern half of the island, which was going to be the main area in which the fighting would occur, to the safer area in the north. About 30,000 old people and children were moved to the north by mid-March 1945, and a further 30,000 when US landings became imminent.

The 32nd Army staff also wished to use as much of the indigenous population as it could in direct support of the war effort, so on 1st January 1945 it ordered total mobilisation. All Okinawan males aged 18–45 were obliged to enter the Japanese service. Some 39,000 were drafted, of whom 15,000 were used

as civilian labourers and 24,000 as rear area troops called the Boeitai (Home Guard). Many of the Boeitai replaced naval battalions and rear-area supply units that had been reorganised and equipped for front line duty.

In addition to these, 1,500 of the senior boys of the middle schools on Okinawa were organised into Blood-and-Iron Volunteer Units and assigned to front-line duty. Some of these students had been tried out in the signal service in the autumn of 1944 with good results, so the program was expanded. Since the autumn of 1944, 600 senior students of the girls' middle schools had also been given basic training as nurses.

Okinawa's economy produced sweet potatoes to feed the cows and pigs, and imported rice from Taiwan to feed the human population. The 32nd Army decided that the livestock would be slaughtered for food and that the populace and military personnel would subsist on the sweet potatoes, thus making the island self-sufficient in food. Replacing rice with sweet potatoes, the poor man's food, was distasteful to soldier and civilian alike for cultural reasons. The 32nd Army went

further and produced alcohol from the sweet potatoes for use as vehicle and truck fuel, at the rate of 300 drums a month.

Main IJA Units – Heavy and Light Divisions

The principal Army units on hand as of March 1945 were 32nd Army headquarters, 24th Infantry Division, 62nd Infantry Division, and 44th Independent Mixed Brigade, together with the 5th Artillery Command and 27th Tank Regiment. In addition to these were some 60 anti-aircraft, machine-gun, and engineering units ranging from battalion to company size. The largest of these was the so-called 11th Shipping Group, whose 19 units boasted some 9,000 men, most of them in Sea Raiding Base Battalions – their role was to send one-man motorboats filled with explosives against the invasion fleet.

The 32nd Army headquarters was itself a formidable force with 7,075 men. Of these, 1,070 were in the headquarters itself, to which were attached 1,912 men in a signals regiment, 204 men in an army hospital, 1,167 men in a field freight depot, and so on. The 32nd Army was formed by IGHQ on 22nd March

1944 as the main command unit for Okinawa. From 11th August 1944, it was commanded by Lieutenant-General Ushijima Mitsuru and based at Naha.

The first of the main combat units to reach Okinawa was the 24th Division, a heavy division. It was organised in December 1939, attached to 32nd Army on 18th July 1944, and disembarked on Okinawa from Manchuria on 5th August 1944. Its commander was Lieutenant-General Amamiya Tatsumi. The 24th, a triangular division with three regiments, three battalions per regiment, and three companies per battalion, was organised and equipped for warfare against mechanised and well-armed Russian forces of the type the IJA clashed with at Nomonhan in 1939. It had abundant combat support units, with artillery, engineer, transport, and reconnaissance elements organic at regimental level. Each regiment, battalion, and company had its own artillery unit, and each battalion also boasted an anti-tank gun company. The transport regiment included three motor transport companies. The 24th, with its firepower, mobility, specialisation, and consistent triangular structure was organised for large-scale operations within a modern army (see Appendix – Tables of Organisation).

Very different from the 24th was the 62nd Division, a light division. The 62nd was formed in June 1943 in Shansi, China; was attached to 32nd Army on 24th July 1944; was concentrated at Shanghai from North China by 13th August 1944; left Shanghai on 16th August; and disembarked at Naha on 19th August. Commanded by Lieutenant-General Fujioka Takeo, the 62nd was based on a proliferation of small autonomous infantry units and little else. It had two brigades, with five battalions per brigade, its 63rd Brigade having five infantry companies per battalion and its 64th Brigade having three infantry companies per battalion. Although it had engineer, medical, and signal units at division level, it had no organic artillery above company level, little firepower, and little mechanised transport. The 62nd Division was really just eight groups of infantry companies, a very light division (see Appendix – Tables of Organisation).

The 62nd Division was so different in concept from the highly structured, heavily equipped 24th Division that it might have belonged to an entirely different army. In fact, it did belong to a different army. The 24th Division had been organised by the Kwantung Army to face Soviet armour on the Manchurian plain shortly after the Nomonhan incident in 1939. The 62nd Division, on the other hand, had been organised by the Central China Expeditionary Army for use as a counter-insurgency force. It was the only major unit to have seen action before Okinawa, but during most of its service its two brigades had

Left: Two US soldiers man the controls of this captured Type 96 twin-barrelled 25mm Japanese anti-aircraft gun. Anti-aircraft batteries were often converted for ground support service as direct fire weapons.

been autonomous and not part of a division at all. In reality, 24th Division was organised to face state-of-the-art Soviet armoured columns in Manchuria, but 62nd Division was organised to fight rural guerrillas in China. These two military tasks were so different that the Japanese army headquarters responsible had evolved completely different organisational structures for their constituent divisions. In the event, of course, the lethal Okinawa battleground would present challenges that resembled neither the mechanised war of the north nor the guerrilla war of the south.

Other Units

The third major combat unit that would fight on Okinawa was the 44th Independent Mixed Brigade, commanded by Major-General Suzuki Shigeki. The 44th IMB was organised on Kyushu, but its headquarters, 2nd Infantry Regiment, brigade artillery, and engineering units were sunk by a US submarine while en route to Okinawa on 29th June 1944. These elements were thus reconstituted between July and September and dispatched again, and this time arrived on Okinawa without loss. The 15th Independent Mixed Regiment was formed on Okinawa on 6th–12th July 1944 by troops airlifted from Japan. It was attached to the 44th IMB on 22nd September 1944. Both the 2nd Infantry Regiment and the 15th Independent Mixed Regiment elements of the 44th IMB were triangular in organisation, with artillery units attached at every level from company up (see Appendix – Tables of Organisation).

Artillery on Okinawa was concentrated under the 5th Artillery Command. The 5th Artillery Command was about brigade size, with 5,100 men. It included, besides its headquarters, four artillery units and three mortar units. The artillery regiments were equipped with 150mm howitzers and 150mm guns. The 1st Independent Artillery Mortar Regiment had 24 x 320mm spigot mortars.

The lavish artillery arrangements were due to the efforts of Colonel Yahara, who had asked IGHQ for the guns and for the 5th Artillery Command to control them. Yahara intended to conceal all the artillery in the centre of the southern defence positions so that all of 32nd Army's firepower could be concentrated at once on any part of the front that might be engaged. Though 32nd Army had far less artillery than the Americans, it could get the maximum effect from what it did have with this organisation. To direct this ambitious project Yahara requested and was sent a noted artillery specialist, Lieutenant-General Wada Kosuke.

The 5th Artillery Command's headquarters, about 150 officers and men, was ordered to Okinawa on 22nd August 1944 and arrived there on 22nd October. The subordinate regiments, some of which came from Japan and others from Manchuria, arrived at various times between July and December.

The only armoured unit that the 32nd Army had was the 27th Tank Regiment of 750 men. The regiment, consisting of a medium tank company with 14 tanks, a light tank company with 13 tanks, a tractor-drawn artillery battery, an infantry company, a maintenance company, and an engineering platoon, arrived on Okinawa from Manchuria on 12th July 1944.

Besides the main line units, there were several independent specialised commands that answered directly to the 32nd Army headquarters, including the 21st Anti-aircraft Artillery Command with its seven anti-aircraft battalions, the 11th Shipping Group with several shipping engineer regiments and sea-raiding battalions, the 19th Air Sector Command that supervised assorted aviation service units, and the 49th Line of Communications Command with several independent motor transport companies. Besides these units, there were four independent machine-gun battalions, four independent anti-tank battalions, and an independent engineer battalion that were parcelled out as needed to the main line units.

The Imperial Japanese Navy (IJN) had almost 9,000 men at the Oroku Naval Air Base adjacent to Naha. Of these, 3,400 were in the Okinawa Naval Base Force and others in various maintenance or construction units. Among the naval units, only the 150 troops in the 81mm mortar battery had been trained for ground fighting prior to arriving in Okinawa. The naval forces, under Rear-Admiral Ota Minoru, were to be under Army jurisdiction once the Americans landed.

Reorganisation
The total strength of the Japanese forces on Okinawa was about 100,000; 67,000 of these were in the IJA, 9,000 were in the IJN, and 24,000 were impressed Okinawans used mostly in service support roles. The strengths of the IJA main units were 32nd

Above: *Well-concealed Japanese gun destroyed by engineers of the US Tenth Army during the American advance. See Fig. 4 page 56.*

Left: *The Type 95 Ha-Go light tank was the best of Japanese armour, but no match for US M4s. This Type 95 – as the 'Under new management' sign indicates – is at an American base in the Central Pacific being used to familiarize US troops with Japanese equipment.*

Army headquarters, 1,070; 32nd Army direct service units, 6,005; 24th Division, 14,360; 62nd Division, 11,623; and 44th IMB, 4,485. These units accounted for only 37,500 of the IJA's 67,000-man complement, however. The remaining 29,000 men were in the specialised anti-aircraft, sea-raiding, and airfield battalions.

It occurred to the 32nd Army staff, however, that these over-manned service units should be reorganised for ground fighting, given the anticipated nature of the coming battle. Between 13th and 20th February 1945, the 1st, 2nd, 3rd, 26th, 27th, 28th, and 29th Sea Raiding Base Battalions were restructured and became the 1st, 2nd, 3rd, 26th, 27th, 28th, and 29th Independent Battalions. By February, these seven battalions' motorboat bases had already been built, and the base forces, each consisting of 900 men, had little to do. Therefore, only motorboat pilot and maintenance companies were left at the bases, and the remaining 600 men in each battalion were withdrawn for use as light infantry battalions. Each independent battalion had three companies of 150 to 180 men, and their men were already trained and equipped with rifles and grenades. To these were added four light machine guns and two heavy grenade launchers per company. The seven independent battalions, about 4,500 troops altogether, were then distributed to the 24th and 62nd Divisions and to the 44th IMB.

On 21st March, 32nd Army staff issued an order that reorganised almost all service support units for ground fighting and placed them under the command of the 62nd and 24th Divisions. The 19th Air Sector Command, for example, became the 1st Specially Established Regiment and was ordered to defend, under the command of the 62nd Division, the Yontan and Kadena airfields it had recently built and maintained.

The 1st Specially Established Brigade was created from units of the 49th Line of Communications Command and placed under that unit's headquarters commander. It consisted of the 2nd, 3rd, and 4th Specially Established Regiments and was made up of line of communications, field ordnance depot, and field freight depot units respectively. It was stationed in the Naha–Yonabaru area under the command of the 62nd Division.

The 2nd Specially Established Brigade was created under the 11th Shipping Group commander. Its 5th and 6th Specially

Established Regiments were drawn from the remainder of the sea raiders and Home Guards, native Okinawans drafted and put in military units, and units of the 11th Shipping Group respectively. The 2nd Specially Established Brigade was stationed on the southwestern end of Okinawa under the command of the 24th Division.

This reorganisation of 21st March added 14,000 men to ground combat strength, leaving only 10,500 of the 67,000 IJA force in specialised service roles. Even among these 10,500, the 3,000 men of the seven anti-aircraft battalions were assigned anti-tank and other direct fire artillery roles on the infantry line once hostilities began. This entailed line use of 70 x 75mm anti-aircraft guns and 100 automatic anti-aircraft guns.

The 9,000 IJN troops on Oroku were also reorganised for ground combat at the end of March. This force was assigned almost entirely to naval and naval air activities. The 13mm and 25mm anti-aircraft batteries in the Okinawa Naval Base Force were able to convert their guns easily for ground support service as direct fire weapons. But these and other naval units suffered from a lack of appropriate infantry equipment, especially individual weapons for the servicemen, as well as from a complete lack of training in ground fighting. Even so, the Oroku force was all reorganised into battalions commanded by naval lieutenants with the companies commanded by sub-lieutenants.

In short, as the battle approached in February and March of 1945, 4,500 men from sea-raiding units, 14,000 men from various shipping and communications units, and 3,000 men from anti-aircraft units, a total of 21,500 men of the 29,000 not already in major line units, were reorganised for potential service on the infantry line. To this total, 9,000 naval troops were also added. Almost all these units were light infantry, however, armed only with rifles and the few machine guns and mortars that the 32nd Army had available to distribute. These units were not trained for infantry fighting, and many of their troops remained in rear-area auxiliary roles until late in the battle when the original line units were badly depleted.

32nd Army's Leadership: Heroism Versus Realism

The individual personalities on an army staff, despite their influence on the outcome of battle, are often forgotten. This was not the case in the IJA 32nd Army. In the 32nd Army staff, two very different sets of principles were present, each represented by a highly placed staff member. The entire strategy of the Okinawa battle on the Japanese side was worked out by the interaction of these two officers' factions and their conflicting policies. Who were the leading lights of the 32nd Army staff, and what strategic principles did they represent?

The 32nd Army commander was Lieutenant-General Ushijima Mitsuru, who was appointed on 8th August 1944 and arrived at his post two days later. This was a routine command rotation; he replaced Lieutenant-General Watanabe Masao, who had been commander since 32nd Army's inception on 22nd March 1944. Ushijima graduated from the Japanese Military Academy (JMA) at Zama in 1908, was a former vice-minister in the Ministry of the Army, and had been an infantry commander in Burma early in the war. In 1944 he was serving as commandant of the Japanese Military Academy. He was a quiet commander who ordinarily approved whatever policy his staff presented to him, who would provide moral support to his subordinates and, if it was necessary, help them reach agreement and resolve differences. He was a typical leader in the mainstream of the Japanese tradition. He did not become embroiled in the disputes that divided the 32nd Army staff but would at times intervene to help to resolve them.

The man with overall responsibility for 32nd Army's day-to-day operations was its chief of staff, Lieutenant-General Cho Isamu (JMA, 1916). Cho had had an extraordinary career. As a

Above: Japanese coastal batteries could prove extremely effective. This is the damage done to USS Longshaw *after being hit by the Japanese batteries near Naha. On the morning of 18th May 1945* Longshaw *ran aground on a coral reef just south of Naha. A tug had just taken her in tow when Japanese shore batteries opened up.* Longshaw's *bow was completely blown off by a hit in the forward magazine, and the battering she took killed 86 of her crew, including the captain. Later in the afternoon,* Longshaw *was destroyed by gunfire and torpedoes from US ships.*

captain in 1930, he had belonged to the right-wing extremist Cherry Society. He was involved in several attempted military coups d'état, including one in October 1931 in which he agreed to become chief of the Tokyo police if the coup succeeded. For his involvement in this episode, he was sent to Manchuria. In 1938, he took part in the clash with Soviet forces at Lake Khasan, near the northeast Korean border, and was involved in some of the negotiations with the Russians. During this period he won fame throughout the IJA by going to sleep on the battlefield. It was said that he strolled from the IJA front line in full view of the Russians and then lay down and went to sleep. His snores were supposedly so loud that they could be clearly heard in both front lines.

In early 1944 Cho was brought from the general headquarters of the Kwantung Army to Tokyo to participate in the projected recapture of Saipan. When IGHQ abandoned that idea on 27th June, it sent him to Okinawa on 1st July to analyse the strategic situation. On 5th July he signaled IGHQ that Okinawa needed three divisions to protect it, plus 30,000 bags of cement for building extensive cave fortifications. These requests may or may not have been prompted by the staff already on Okinawa, but they did conform closely to the main outlines of actual defence arrangements later. In any case Cho was appointed chief of staff of the 32nd Army on 8th July 1944.

Cho was a heavy drinker and when intoxicated would perform a dance with his samurai sword. He liked having fine cuisine as well as good Scotch whisky in his headquarters. He was enthusiastic and communicated that enthusiasm to those around him. He harboured strong resentments against those

who crossed him, but only for a very short time. In short he was a man of strong feelings and aggressive personality who utterly believed in his cause and in the capabilities of the IJA. He also tended to base strategic judgments on his enthusiasms rather than on a cool appreciation of reality.

Cho's chief subordinate was the senior operations officer, Colonel Yahara Hiromichi (JMA, 1923). Yahara had been with the 32nd Army since its inception on 22nd March 1944 and prior to that had attended the IJA's War College; before the war he served ten months at Fort Moultrie in the United States; later served as a staff officer in China, Malaya, and Burma; and taught at the JMA. By personality and inclination he was the opposite of Cho. He was seen by colleagues as introspective and aloof but good at his business, which was crafting operations. For him war was a science whose practice demanded cool rationality. When Cho was made Yahara's superior on 8 July, there was some soul-searching among the IGHQ staff as to whether that was a good idea, but the staff eventually decided it was.

In the event, Yahara and Cho would often have different views on what operations should be carried out, with the rest of the 32nd Army staff supporting one or the other. The two men had very different assumptions about the nature of ground combat and what factors were most important in determining its outcome. Observing the drama between Cho and Yahara were the headquarters staff, who, by consensus, decided to support either one or the other: they were the six lieutenant-colonels and majors on the central staff of 32nd Army who were privy to the main operational decisions, as well as four colonels and a major who headed weapons, administration, medical, and legal branches of the 32nd Army headquarters (see Appendix – Tables of Organisation).

The Centre of Authority in the 32nd Army Staff

IJA staffs did not reach decisions in the same manner as US Army staffs. In the US Army, a unit commander would hear the evidence from his staff, then decide on a course of action. In the IJA, however, unit commanders had only a symbolic function. The commander was expected only to carry the burden of spiritual responsibility on his shoulders, manage contacts between his unit and superiors, and offer moral support to his subordinates. Practical responsibility for the unit as a whole lay in the hands of its chief of staff. Tasks relating to operations were delegated to the senior staff officer, whose position was similar

to a US Army G.3 but who had far more influence than his US counterpart because of the commander's passive role. When trying to arrive at an operational decision, the rest of the staff was expected to provide information and insights and to discuss the issue at hand in the framework of a staff meeting. The chief of staff would articulate the policy chosen, and then the whole staff was supposed to agree by consensus that the course chosen was right. The senior staff officer would then draw up the plans and oversee their implementation.

Compared to American practice, this system gave more power to the staff, especially the junior members, and meant that staff discussions tended to shape more directly the content of command decisions. The commander himself was aware of the issues and was present at staff meetings to bless the results, but ordinarily he did not intervene as long as the decision making process was working. These unique IJA staff practices sprang in part from the German example, which had been influential in the IJA's early years, and in part from indigenous traditions of consensus decision making. In the Okinawa campaign, these practices governed the staff-meeting system in which crucial decisions were reached in a struggle of words between Cho and Yahara.

Above: A bomb churns up the water near a Japanese midget submarine and torpedo boat base in a sheltered cove on Okinawa. US aircraft pounded Okinawa for nine days before the landings.

Above left: The Kerama Islands, some 25 miles west of Okinawa, were invaded on 26th March 1945. This photographs shows men of 1st Battalion, 306th Infantry Regiment, 77th Division, during the fighting.

Ground or Air

In March 1945, 32nd Army requested that IGHQ allow the destruction of the Yontan and Kadena airfields on the grounds that the airfields were impossible to defend. A brigade could delay their seizure for no more than several days and then only at the cost of thousands of lives. Therefore, 32nd Army argued, it was better to destroy the airfields; this would deny their use to the enemy, at no cost of life, for at least ten days, which was how long, the 32nd Army calculated, it would take the Americans to rebuild them. IGHQ approved the request, so destruction began on 10th March 1945 'using the air units in the area' and was largely completed by the end of the month.

Above: *An Australian Army officer inspects a Japanese 37mm Type 94 infantry rapid-fire gun captured during the Allied advance in New Guinea.*

Right: *From the start of the campaign against the Japanese in the Pacific it was obvious that amphibious operations were going to need purpose-built vessels capable of delivering large numbers of troops, their equipment, transport, heavy weapons and logistic support to the battlefield. By the time of Okinawa, the range of amphibious warfare vessels included landing craft (LCI for infantry, LCS for support, LCT for tank), landing ships such as this LST (landing ship tank) carrying 77th Infantry Division to Ie, and the ubiquitous DUKWs and Amtracs.*

Destroying the airfields marked a dramatic turnaround of IGHQ's earlier policy. Prior to this time IGHQ had expected the defence of Okinawa to be accomplished mainly by air power and had envisioned Okinawa as a giant air-base complex. In this, IGHQ had been at odds with the 32nd Army staff from the beginning. The 32nd Army, expecting imminent American landings, saw Okinawa in terms of a land-based defence. It had no confidence that Japanese air power would have the desired effect of limiting the American advance to the island, let alone the assault on it.

IGHQ, on the other hand, under its TEI-Go plan of April–July 1944 saw Okinawa only as an air base to help defend the Marianas line. Under the SHO-Go plan of July–November 1944, which recognised the need for ground defence of Okinawa, it was still assumed that many of the invading Americans would be stopped in the water by the 1,500 suicide

planes gathered for that purpose in China, Taiwan, and the Philippines. Even the SHO-Go plans of November 1944–April 1945 still laid heavy emphasis on the use of suicide air attacks against the US fleet, albeit launched from Kyushu and Taiwan, not Okinawa. The 32nd Army and Yahara felt that this air-oriented policy, which built airfields without protecting them, was tantamount to building airfields for the enemy.

From July and August 1944 Cho and Yahara, from their vantage point on Okinawa, were doubtful of the efficacy of Japanese air power and directed all the energies of their main units, which were just arriving, to building fortifications. The building of airfields, IGHQ's priority, was left to Okinawan labourers. During August 1944, IGHQ sent several emissaries of lieutenant-general rank to Okinawa to inspect the airfields' progress. When the pace was discovered to be slow, they severely castigated Cho and threatened to dissolve the whole 32nd Army staff. Faced with this eventuality, Cho finally did devote enough resources to building the airfields so that they were, in the main, completed by the end of September 1944.

When the 44th IMB withdrew from the Hagushi plain in February 1945, leaving Yontan and Kadena airfields unprotected, the 6th Air Army, the formation of 10th Area Army on Taiwan responsible for Okinawa's air defence, complained bitterly. The 32nd Army asked for more troops if it had to defend the airfields, this was denied. A compromise was worked out with IGHQ whereby 32nd Army was permitted to attempt to prevent American use of the airfields by long-range artillery fire. On the other hand, the 32nd Army wished to have a number of suicide attack planes based on Okinawa to strike the US fleet when it came within 60 miles. IGHQ promised 32nd Army 300 planes for this, but this promise failed to materialise and few planes were actually available when the American landings started.

Throughout the long period of waiting, March 1944 to March 1945, IGHQ relied on an air strategy that assumed abundant supplies and equipment would be available. But the strategy became increasingly implausible as time went by, especially to the 32nd Army staff, who knew what had happened on Saipan and Iwo Jima and who also knew the outcomes of the air battles of the Philippine Sea and of Taiwan. For IGHQ to reverse its policy at the eleventh hour, early March 1945, meant that in the end even IGHQ recognised that an air defence strategy was hopeless and that Okinawa would have to be held by fighting on the ground. Reliance on air power to avoid a decisive encounter on the ground had proved to be a fantasy, a fantasy appreciated first by the ground officers in the area about to be attacked.

Chapter 2 Defensive Engagement, April 1945

By the end of March, 32nd Army was fairly well prepared to resist invasion, although a last-minute personnel shuffle disrupted unit cohesion. The US preparatory bombardment soon began. On 23rd March 1945, American carrier planes bombed Okinawa and, from 24th March, a preparatory naval bombardment rained down 13,000 16-inch and 6-inch shells. This bombardment had no specific targets, however, and amounted to little more than an initial warning of the strength of American firepower. The 32nd Army's concealment had been so effective that, despite daily aerial reconnaissance, the American gunnery spotters did not know where on the island the enemy positions were.

On 26th March, American forces invaded and captured the Kerama Islands, 60 miles west of Naha. The Japanese went to 'War Preparations A', that is to say full alert. The few kamikaze aircraft that were available on Okinawa sortied from Kadena airfield on 27th, 28th, and 29th March and damaged a few of the American ships. To raise morale, Lieutenant-General Cho put up a sign next to the 32nd Army headquarters cave that read 'Heaven's Grotto Battle Headquarters', a light-hearted reference to a myth about the Japanese nation's foundation. What really raised morale, however, was that the arduously constructed cave fortresses had protected their occupants against the 16-inch naval shells. Until the shelling began, the Japanese staff and soldiers had not been sure whether their caves would really protect them.

The American Landings

At 08:30 on 1st April 1945, US forces began to land on the Hagushi beaches (see map 4). The 32nd Army believed there was a fifty-fifty chance that the Americans would land there rather than at Itoman or Minatoga. The Japanese believed the Americans would land in one place, or two at the most, since that is what the

Americans had done in their previous operations. According to their long-standing plan, the Japanese refrained both from firing their artillery on the American beachhead and from responding to the aerial reconnaissance activities. The Americans did not expect such passivity since, even at Iwo Jima, the Japanese had directed artillery fire against the beaches.

The main units of 32nd Army did not stir from their underground positions in the south. Meeting the Americans around the Yontan and Kadena airfields, however, was the IJA 1st Specially Established Regiment, a unit that had only recently been formed and had little combat training. The Americans captured both airfields on the first day, a disappointment to the 32nd Army staff. The 1st Specially Established Regiment suffered heavy losses and retreated to the north, where it combined with the Kunigami Detachment, under whose command it had been placed on 2nd April.

Amphibious Landings

The tactics involved in landings against Japanese-occupied islands evolved quickly during 1942–44; by 1945 they were well-defined. Air and sea bombardments would attempt to destroy fixed positions, aircraft, airfields and gun emplacements; smokescreens would sometimes be used to cover the approaching ships; then the initial waves would be ferried in using Amtracs – the LVT (landing vehicle tracked) series of which over 18,500 of all types would see action with US forces.

Above: *Ships make smoke during the attack on the Keramas, 26th April.*

Below left: *Battleship USS* Tennessee *(BB-43) bombards Okinawa just before H-Hour on 1st April, part of the heaviest naval bombardment of the war in support of a landing – 44,825 rounds of gunfire, 32,000 rockets and 22,500 mortar shells pounded the Japanese before the Amtracs went in.*

Below: *Amtracs and troops advance toward the shores of Tokashiki in the Keramas.*

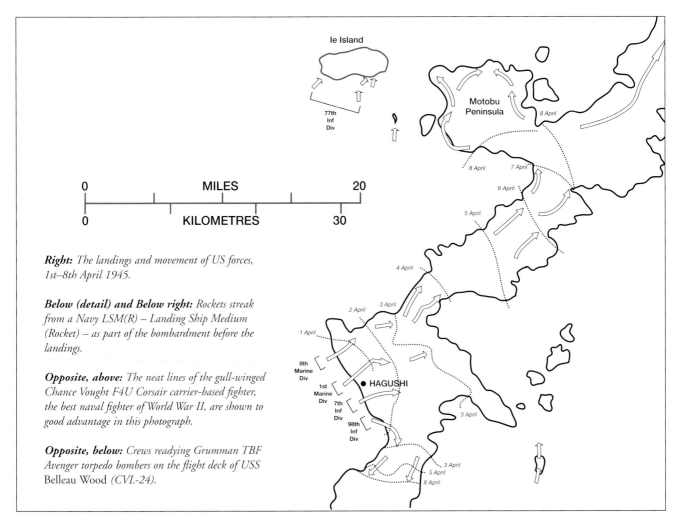

Ie Island

77th
Inf
Div

Motobu
Peninsula

8 April

8 April

7 April

6 April

5 April

4 April

3 April

2 April

1 April

8th
Marine
Div

1st
Marine
Div

7th
Inf
Div

98th
Inf
Div

● HAGUSHI

3 April

3 April

5 April

8 April

Right: The landings and movement of US forces,
1st–8th April 1945.

Below (detail) and Below right: Rockets streak
from a Navy LSM(R) – Landing Ship Medium
(Rocket) – as part of the bombardment before the
landings.

Opposite, above: The neat lines of the gull-winged
Chance Vought F4U Corsair carrier-based fighter,
the best naval fighter of World War II, are shown to
good advantage in this photograph.

Opposite, below: Crews readying Grumman TBF
Avenger torpedo bombers on the flight deck of USS
Belleau Wood (CVL-24).

Right: USS Eastland *(APA-163) and* LST-622 *off Okinawa. Eastland was one of the 119-strong 'Haskell' class amphibious attack transports, all completed and commissioned in 1944–45 and used mainly in the final push across the Pacific. The class had a crew of 56 officers and 480 enlisted men and could carry 86 officers 1,475 enlisted men; cargo to the capacity of 150,000cu. ft; and two LCMs, 12 LCVPs and three LCPUs. Eastland arriving at the Keramas on 26th March, landed her troops without opposition on Yakabi Shima and remained in the archipelago until 26th April.*

Below right: Troops of 77th Infantry Division advancing inland on Tokashiki, one of the Kerama Islands. Note in the centre of the photograph the bazooka – these hand-held weapons provided the infantry with mobile 'bunker-busters' in terrain or weather conditions that tanks or mobile artillery found impossible.*

Below: This aerial view of US invasion ships shows the difference in size between the LSTs (the seven to the right that include 1015, 1030, 926, 227, 687, 894) and the much smaller LCTs (792 and, just visible at extreme left of the frame, 1179) on the beach at Okinawa.*

Above: Amtracs coming ashore to an unopposed landing, 1st April.

Above right: Aerial view of US tanks sweeping through Yontan Airfield, while American gunners are already manning anti-aircraft installations. By the end of the first day both the airfields nearest the landing beaches – Kadena and Yontan – had been captured with few US casualties.

The 32nd Army had left no forces to the north of the Hagushi beaches except for the Kunigami Detachment, whose orders were to delay the American advance while retiring northward. (A Japanese unit which was organised to undertake a particular role or action, which was less than brigade size was usually named after its commander, though in this case it was named after a place, north Okinawa. Such a detachment was usually either organised around two or more regiments, or a single regiment, or even a battalion. The Japanese also used permanent brigades and regiments also organised for a particular role, with organic artillery, transport, signals, and other support units, which were then referred to as 'independent mixed brigades' and 'independent mixed regiments.') The Kunigami Detachment in northern Okinawa consisted of the 44th IMB's 2nd Infantry Regiment less its 3rd Battalion, a force of about 1,715 men, (see Appendix – Tables of Organisation).

With the Americans on the Hagushi beaches now easily expanding their beachhead in advances both northwards and south, the 32nd Army staff formulated a series of attacks to push them back. But, for reasons not known, the Japanese forces either failed to carry them out or those that were undertaken were limited as soon as they was made. The 10th Area Army on Taiwan and IGHQ in Tokyo pressured 32nd Army to attack and recapture the Yontan and Kadena airfields. IGHQ communicated with 32nd Army by radio. This advice was really unnecessary, however, since attack as a battle tactic was the predominant feature of Japanese infantry doctrine. The aggressive attack was supposed to catch the enemy off guard and force an early outcome. Night infiltration and close combat were supposed to offset the enemy's advantage in firepower. Attack would overcome all problems. The 32nd Army staff, echoing IGHQ's wishes, repeatedly advocated attacking American lines in the early days of April.

Having been encouraged by a signal from the 10th Area Army to attack and fearing that commanding general Ushijima's reputation would suffer if an attack were not made, chief of staff Cho called a staff conference on the night of 3rd April. He said the US position was still not fully established. Therefore, to annihilate this enemy, 32nd Army should make a general attack

immediately, relying on night infiltration and close combat, the form of fighting the IJA believed it excelled in, to gain an advantage over the Americans.

Cho then canvassed the members of the army staff one by one to see if they agreed. The staff officers were of course junior to Cho in rank and age, being only lieutenant-colonels and majors and anything from eight to 20 years younger. These younger officers, one after another, enthusiastically agreed with Cho's suggestion, since it represented standard IJA doctrine and also their superior was expecting them to support him. Major Jin Naomichi approved of the plan even more emphatically than the others because he was the aviation staff officer and so was eager to retake the airfields because of their importance for IGHQ's larger air and sea strategy. Only Major Nagano Hideo, an assistant operations officer, somewhat qualified his approval.

But in this atmosphere of total agreement, as Operations Officer Colonel Yahara vigorously attacked the proposal. He spoke with the intensity of a man who knew he was right. He said that the young staff officers were agreeing to Cho's suggestions in a cursory manner, as if it were just a five minute question in the military academy exam. He said they knew nothing of the terrain or other particular factors affecting the attack, even though this data was critical and had actually been

gathered by Cho's subordinates. Yahara said they were making policy in an erratic and random manner. Yahara also pointed out that they were abandoning the policy of fighting a campaign of attrition, which had been carefully developed since the preceding autumn. Moreover, if they thought the Americans would be caught unprepared, that was 'a complete fantasy'. The Americans were already established on the beachhead; they were now advancing in an orderly way both to the north and also to the south, and would be still better organised after the three days it would take the Japanese to prepare a large-scale attack. Moving in the open under American guns would be suicidal and wreck 32nd Army in a few days, which would be especially disheartening given the length of time and the effort that had been made in preparing the elaborate tunnel positions. Besides that, he suggested, the radioed order from 10th Area Army for attack was not absolutely explicit, leaving local commanders some latitude to disregard it if doing so was in the army's interest, taking account of the local circumstances.

Cho heard this critical statement to the end without interruption. When Yahara had finished his argument, Cho stood up and deliberately announced that the consensus of the meeting was that the staff favoured attack. He adjourned the meeting for 30 minutes, after which it was reconvened in

Above and Above right: The largest, most heavily armed and armoured battleships of World War II were the Yamato *and* Musashi. *Weighing 64,000 tons, carrying nine 18-inch guns and with armour 25 inches thick in places, both were sunk by carrier-based aircraft –* Musashi *in the Sibuyan Sea on 24th October 1944 and* Yamato *on a kamikaze mission in April 1945 en route for Okinawa. With only enough fuel to get to Okinawa, the plan was that* Yamato *would beach herself on the island and then provide heavy artillery support to the defenders. Discovered, she was pounded by bombs and torpedoes and eventually sank on 6th April – the so-called 'last sortie of the Imperial Japanese Navy'. The photographs show a debriefing of a US pilot involved in the attack – Lieutenant (j.g.) G. D. Rogers of the* Bennington *– and the* Yamato *taking a bomb hit.*

Lieutenant-General Ushijima's office, to hear their commander request an attack by the main body of the army on the Yontan and Kadena airfields. A general attack was now the army's stated intention, and an attack plan six paragraphs in length was drafted.

Yahara was very upset over this impending waste, not only of the 32nd Army but also of the past eight months of his own labours. Yahara therefore sought to lobby the various division commanders when they were briefed on the attack orders on 4th April. He urged each of them to voice opposition to the plan and did persuade one of them to do so. The orders, however, remained in force.

The attack was not scheduled until 6th April, however, and on the night of 4th April an air unit reported to 32nd Army that an American task force of three aircraft carriers and 50 transports and cargo vessels had been spotted 90 miles south of Naha. If the Americans landed at Machinato airfield, just behind the existing forward line, at the same moment as the Japanese attack, the result would be catastrophic. Yahara seized on this message and took it to Cho, who summarily cancelled the offensive that had caused the 32nd Army staff so much turmoil for the last several days.

Although Yahara seemed to be a minority of one in the argument over the attack, and had coolly discarded 30 years of IJA doctrine in adopting his position, nevertheless his point of view prevailed in the end. The 6th April offensive was cancelled. This argument over the proposed attack was significant because most of 32nd Army's decisions for the rest of its existence would be reached in this same turbulent way, by a test of wills and words between Cho and Yahara.

The two men had different personalities. Cho was famous for physical courage, spontaneous decision, and a robust presence that inspired confidence and friendship. Yahara was known as a sour, aloof, preoccupied intellectual. The disputes between them pitted romantic aspiration against reality and rosy doctrine against harsh fact. The most surprising feature of this turbulent decision-making process, however, was that most observers felt it produced good decisions.

Planning the Japanese 12th April Offensive

From the earliest days of the American presence up until the major Japanese offensive of 4th May, there was a continuing tendency in 32nd Army to go over to the attack, with Yahara in every case trying to stem the tide. The attack impulse came from higher headquarters as well as from doctrinal habit, since the staffs of 10th Area Army on Taiwan and of IGHQ in Tokyo couched their expectations in terms of their strategic goals rather than in terms of the realities of the Okinawa battlefield.

On the night of 5th April, when 10th Area Army heard that the 6th April offensive had been cancelled, it immediately signaled to the 32nd Army that it must attack on the night of 8th April to recapture the airfields. This time the message was a specific command. Consequently, Ushijima's response was to issue an order for a general attack for the night of 8th April, the order's text being similar to that of the attack planned for the 6th.

Once again, on the afternoon of 7th April, an American naval group was observed moving west of Naha, causing fears of an American landing near Machinato and an advance toward the village of Urasoe, which was behind the left flank of the Japanese main line. Cho therefore modified the attack orders into a night sortie which was to be carried out by two companies, a gesture which had little effect.

When no landings materialised, on 8th April Cho instructed Yahara prepare a night attack for 12th April. A brigade or more would cross US lines, and small units would penetrate deeply behind the American positions. If successful, a general attack would follow immediately. Two young staff officers, Kimura and Kusumaru, who had served in China, thought it was possible to make a movement at night to the depth of six miles. Yahara thought it was the height of folly but prepared the plan in his usual businesslike way.

The American Advance

Meanwhile, the Americans had landed four divisions onto the Hagushi beaches (see map 4). By 3rd April they had secured most of the area of Hagushi, and their southern perimeter had crossed the isthmus. By 8th April, the Americans had pushed the Kunigami Detachment northward as far as the Motobu Peninsula and the Gaya Detachment southward back into the Japanese main line. The Gaya Detachment was a small force sent out, like its counterpart the Kunigami, to delay the US advance.

The US 1st and 6th Marine Divisions were able to secure all of Motobu Peninsula by 20th April, despite stubborn resistance by remnants of the Kunigami Detachment on Yae-Take Mountain. This meant that the two-thirds of Okinawa north of the Hagushi beachhead was all essentially subdued by that date. Only a few soldiers of the Kunigami Detachment remained in the hills until the end of the campaign. Meanwhile on Ie Island, from 16th to 22nd April, the US 77th Infantry Division had

The Taking of Ie Jima

The island of Ie lies about 3.5 miles off Okinawa. Its most prominent feature is the Pinnacle which was heavily fortified, as were the caves in the sea cliffs. At dawn on 16th April two battleships, four cruisers and seven destroyers of the Fifth Fleet started a heavy bombardment; the Amtracs and landing craft followed and soon 77th Division infantry were fighting on the beaches. Nevertheless it would take four days of bloody conflict before Ie Jima fell.

Above: *Infantry preparing to advance.*

Above left: *Ernie Pyle, a noted war correspondent, was shot by a sniper on Ie. Because he lived with the soldiers in the field and reported what he saw first hand, he was well liked by the GIs. Here he is seen signing autographs. A marker was raised to him with the inscription: 'At this spot the 77th Infantry Division lost a buddy. Ernie Pyle 18 April 1945'.*

Left: *The beaches of Ie Jima – note Pinnacle on the right.*

Opposite, above: *Rockets fired toward the Pinnacle. Beyond, to the south, are the town of Ie and Government House, almost obscured by smoke from the pre-invasion bombardment.*

Opposite, below: *Aerial view of Ie Jima showing the airstrip. In spite of the Japanese attempts to render it unusable, 507th Fighter Group flew P-47 missions from the strip from 1st July through 15th August.*

destroyed the defending troops who were from a unit of the Kunigami Detachment.

However, the advance of the Americans toward the south halted for the moment on 8th April. The main struggle on Okinawa would take place on the southern isthmus where, on 8th April, the US 7th and 96th Infantry Divisions had only just reached the main Japanese line for the first time. This happened while the Japanese were still debating whether to attack, and it had two important consequences for the Japanese operational situation. One was that the units of the IJA 62nd Division that manned the main line were engaged and could not easily be deployed for an attack. The other was that now it was not necessary to attack to achieve the close combat IJA favoured, because the Americans had obligingly moved forward.

The Japanese 12th April Offensive

The US 7th and 96th Infantry Divisions kept steady pressure on the Japanese isthmus line from 9th April onwards, while preparing for a major offensive thrust that would begin on 19th April. At the 32nd Army staff headquarters, the plans for the Japanese 12th April attacks went forward. The units of the IJA 62nd Division which were already on the isthmus line were to hold their positions. The IJA 22nd Infantry Regiment was to be brought north from the Oroku area, placed under 62nd Division's command, and assembled northeast of Shuri. At sunset, the 22nd Regiment was to attack through the US lines on the east of the Ginowan Road, then advance as far as Shimabuku (see map 5).

The 62nd Division was to use three reserve battalions from its own rear areas, the 23rd, 272nd, and 273rd, for the assault which was to take place at sunset. The 273rd Battalion was to attack along the west coast, the 272nd was to advance along the west side of the Ginowan Road, and the 23rd was to move forward between them. The 32nd Army artillery was to provide covering fire beginning at sunset, with barrages briefly directed at the American line, then it would be shifted to American rear areas.

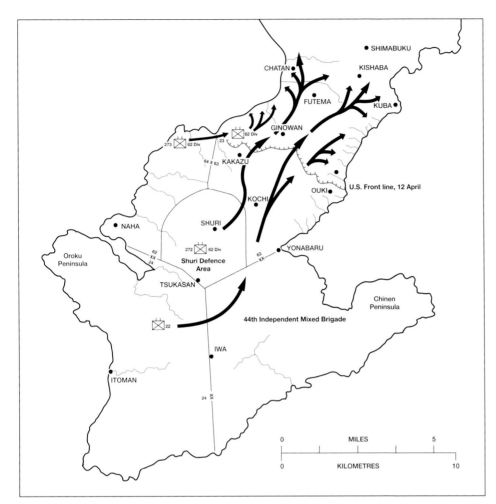

Far left: Two M4s were knocked out on Ie Jima's 'Bloody Ridge' by artillery fire from the Pinnacle. In total US forces suffered 172 killed in action, 902 wounded and 46 missing during the battle, as well as five tanks.

Left: Plan for the IJA's 12th April offensive.

The orders drafted by Yahara were handed to subordinate commands on the night of 10th April and were carried out as planned on the evening of 12th April. In the event, the assault unit on the right of the attack, the 22nd Infantry Regiment, failed to move forward because of unfamiliar terrain or perhaps it simply got lost in the darkness. The 23rd and 272nd Battalions, moving on the west side of the Ginowan Road, penetrated 1,000 yards behind the US lines but were isolated after dawn on 13th April. When these units retreated into the Japanese lines that night, only half of their men had survived. The 273rd Battalion, moving up the west coast, fared worse still since the entire unit was lost.

Given the poor results, Ushijima ordered the offensive suspended on 13th April. Moreover, it emerged that Yahara had told the 62nd Division commander to commit only a few troops to the attack since it was bound to fail. Though events proved Yahara right, his conduct has been criticised as undermining the normal structure of command.

Night Problems

The night attacks suffered from several unexpected problems. Heavy shelling had changed the landscape, blasting away villages and thickets, so that even though night infiltrators knew their maps and thought they knew the terrain, they lacked the landmarks needed to tell them where they actually were. Moreover, frequent illumination shells forced the eyes of night infiltrators to adjust so many times that their capacity to adjust was lost. They became temporarily blinded and so were unable to move.

Because of the unfamiliar terrain and flash blindness, the Japanese night fighters had difficulty reaching their assigned objectives. In fact, it was hard for them to reach their jumping-off points. Continuous naval bombardment of crossroads and bridges forced units to rush across in small groups between shells so that the units became strung out on the roads and difficult to control. It was hard to move heavy ammunition and supplies forward because of these interdiction points and the generally churned up roads. Even when units reached their northward assembly points safely by night, they were immediately exposed to aerial observation and artillery fire at dawn, since they lacked enough time to dig in. Units that attacked across American lines safely in darkness had the same problem; they lacked time to dig in and so were utterly exposed to artillery fire at morning light. Night attacks, like flanking manoeuvres, were a kind of cure-all in pre-war Japanese doctrine. But they failed to provide the expeditious results on Okinawa that IJA doctrine had led the 32nd Army staff to expect.

Moving the Army North

On 19th April, US Army's XXIV Corps launched the major offensive it had been preparing for ten days along the whole Kakazu–Ouki line (see map 6). The IJA 62nd Division, which held this line and had suffered in the 12th April attacks, was becoming increasingly weakened, to the point where the whole 32nd Army staff agreed it would soon collapse. The division had already been ordered, after the 12th April offensive, to put its reserve units on the line so that each of its thinned battalions could shorten its front. By 19th April, the 62nd Division had lost 35 per cent of its personnel and 39 per cent of its artillery.

After four days of the new American offensive, 62nd Division still held firm but had been pushed back half a mile from its 19th April positions. In hard fighting it had relinquished Nishibaru Ridge in the centre and the neighbouring ridges on its right. The 62nd Division was most undermined, however, by the US 27th Infantry Division's penetration on the Japanese left. By aggressive and persistent advances, the 27th had thrust a salient into the Japanese line just east of Gusukuma village, thus isolating the Japanese forces on the western coastal heights from the rest of the Japanese line.

By 22nd April, the IJA 62nd Division had lost half of its original strength and its line was nearly broken through on the left. Yahara was in a quandary over this. He estimated that for every battalion, field gun, and mortar the 62nd Division had on the line, the US XXIV Corps had four, not to mention the 100 tanks and 640 aircraft Yahara calculated to be at XXIV Corps' disposal.

In pondering the Americans' next move, however, Yahara's constant preoccupation was his judgement that the US Tenth Army had six divisions ashore, of which only the 27th, 96th, and 7th Infantry Divisions were deployed on the Kakazu–Ouki line. As he considered the operational facts from the American viewpoint, Yahara was convinced that it was in the Americans' best interest to use amphibious envelopment and land a force of a division or more on Okinawa's southeast coast at Minatoga.

This would force Japanese combat units to fight on two fronts and could lead to an early collapse of the over-extended Japanese perimeter. The US Tenth Army did, in fact, send escorted transports to the Minatoga coast on 19th April to threaten a landing.

For the IJA 24th Division to be facing the southwest coast and the 44th IMB to be facing the southeast coast was an ideal arrangement to counter a second American front, but they could not be left there because the 62nd Division line in the north was itself about to disintegrate. So Yahara developed two alternatives to the present Japanese dispositions. One was to move the 24th Division and 44th IMB to the north to reinforce the 62nd Division line. The other alternative was to abandon the northern line and draw the 32nd Army into three strongpoints in the Shuri, Kiyan, and Chinen areas. Both approaches would shorten the perimeter being defended.

Yahara felt on the whole that moving the bulk of IJA forces to the northern line was the sounder course, but he was still dismayed by the prospect of an American landing in the rear. He was so uncertain that he took all of these problems to Lieutenant-General Cho on 22nd April and asked him what to do. It is a measure of his consternation that this was the only time he ever consulted Cho about operations.

Cho said without hesitation that the 32nd Army would be lost if the 62nd Division were not reinforced immediately, so 24th Division and 44th IMB must be moved north for that purpose. If the Americans landed in the south, the Japanese would address that when it happened. 'A man who chases two rabbits won't catch either one', he added, quoting a well-known

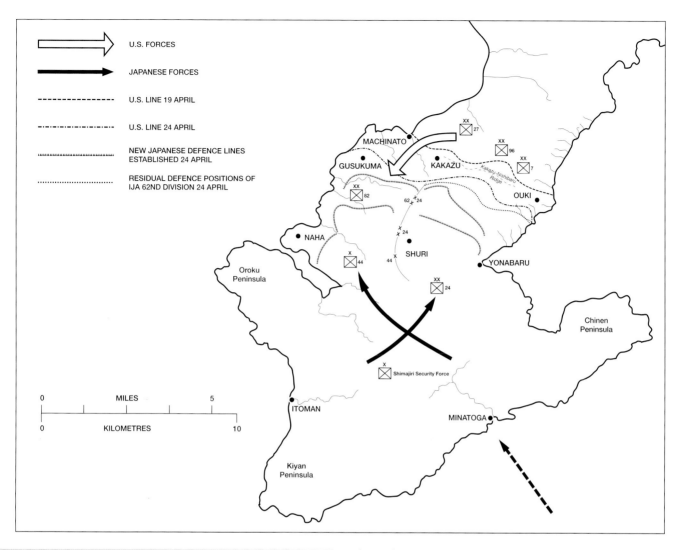

Above: The IJA positions as of 25th April 1945.

Left: American infantrymen move inland from the invasion beaches as smoke from the battleship bombardment rises from the distant hills.

Japanese proverb. Cho's decision was quick and clear, which made moving the troops north seem to be obviously the right course. Cho had a decisive confidence and radiated this to the staff around him. His cutting of the knot put Yahara's tormented mind at ease. To reach the right answers quickly without worrying about them too much was Cho's forte. Yahara was grateful.

Since the 62nd Division line was in such bad shape, Yahara decided to use only part of the reinforcements, elements of the 24th Division, to take over the right half of the 62nd Division's line, while using the rest of the reinforcements to form a solid,

Above: Commanding generals of various forces and Vice Admiral Harry W. Hill meet at the US Tenth Army headquarters on Okinawa. They are, from left to right: Brigadier General E. D. Post, Lieutenant General Roy S. Geiger, Lieutenant General Robert C. Richardson, Jr., Vice Admiral Hill, Major General Fred C. Wallace, Major General Louis A. Woods, USMC and Major General John R. Hodge.

Above right: From left to right: Lientenant General Simon Bolivar Buckner, Jr., Vice Admiral Richmond Kelley Turner, USN, and Brigadier General Oliver P. Smith, USMC, aboard Turner's flagship, planning the invasion of Okinawa.

fresh defence line a mile to the rear. The 24th Division was to hold the line from Shuri eastward and the 44th IMB was to hold it from Shuri westward, deploying behind the 62nd Division. This would allow defence of the forward line to be continuous and, at the same time, provide a strong defensive position in the rear into which retreating forces could fall back gradually. The southern areas would be manned only by a so-called Shimajiri Security Force of 5,500 men, created out of rear-area supply units. Its job was to delay any American thrust from the south until main-force units could return to the area.

By the night of 24th April, the 24th Division and the 44th IMB had moved into their new northern positions. The American forces were completely unaware of the night movements of these units. In the next few days, however, Japanese soldiers on the line were seen with 24th Division markings, revealing to the Americans that at least some of the 24th Division had moved up from the south. For the Americans, IJA operations on the northern line continued essentially unchanged. They remained unaware that the Japanese had faced a grave operational dilemma. To US Tenth Army, all that could be seen was that the Japanese front line was continuing to resist their attacks.

Even so, the US Tenth Army actually was considering whether to land on the Minatoga coast at almost the same moment Yahara was agonising over that possibility. The idea was advanced not by the US Tenth Army staff but by field commanders of the units that had not been engaged in the fighting. Major General Andrew Bruce, commander of the US 77th Infantry Division, urged that his division be landed on the Minatoga beaches, behind the Japanese main line, rather than merely being fed into line in the north. The 77th Infantry Division had had success with such a manoeuvre on Leyte when

it landed at Ormoc behind Japanese lines. Yahara was also aware of the recent Leyte operation.

Lieutenant General Simon Bolivar Buckner and the US Tenth Army staff rejected Bruce's request, however, on the grounds that the Minatoga beaches were too constricted to stage supplies and ordnance adequately, for even a single division. The steep terrain near the beaches favoured the defence, and any unit there would be isolated. It might be more like Anzio than Leyte, he suggested. Besides that, the three divisions on the line needed to be relieved, and Buckner's three unused divisions would all be needed there. When it was determined about 26th April that the entire IJA 24th Division was on the northern line, Major General John R. Hodge, commander of XXIV Corps, went to the US Tenth Army staff and advocated a landing at Minatoga, as Major General Bruce had, since Japanese defences there were thin. The Tenth Army staff officers again rejected the proposal, just as Buckner had a few days before, and for similar reasons.

Buckner's decision not to open a second front in the south was, and remains, controversial. It is still not clear whether a division landed at Minatoga would have caused the Japanese perimeter to collapse early, or merely have caused the battle of attrition to be continued on another front and on different terrain, or even have resulted in a US division being pinned down on a hostile beach. The calculations of the Tenth Army staff may have been correct. The Japanese forces, even at the end of May, were still able to move the six miles between northern and southern fronts both unobserved and speedily. The US forces at Minatoga would have had no developed rear areas to draw on and would soon have faced defence caves re-occupied by the IJA 24th Division. The IJA 5th Artillery Command, placed on interior lines, could have brought its full weight to bear on Minatoga without moving away from the northern front. But the US XXIV Corps artillery, located north of the Shuri line, could not have reached Minatoga to cover a US division there, though abundant naval artillery could have been used. All in all, Buckner's judgment may have been right.

Yahara had trouble anticipating Buckner's decision because of two considerations that loomed large for Buckner but not for Yahara. One was that Buckner's staff members had a practical sense of the terrain needed to support the Americans' high volumes of logistics so that they, but not Yahara, could see that suitable conditions did not exist at Minatoga. The other factor was that Buckner was aware of how tired American line units were becoming in continuous combat on the isthmus line, something that had not occurred to Yahara.

Above: *Lieutenant General Buckner (right), commander of the US Tenth Army, confers with Major General John R. Hodge commander of the US Army's 24th Corps, at an advanced headquarters on Okinawa.*

Left: *General Joseph W. Stillwell confers with General Buckner at Buckner's headquarters, shortly before his death on Okinawa.*

Far left: *From a rocky ledge observation post, three American generals watch US troops advance towards Naha. Left to right are: General Buckner, Major General Lemuel C. Shepherd, commander of the Sixth Marine Division and Brigadier General William T. Clement, General Shepherd's assistant division commander.*

Chapter 3 Lethality in Motion: Tactics

The fighting on Okinawa had features that were all its own, but even so its dynamics bore a startling resemblance to the fierce no-man's-land fighting of World War I. The conditions of warfare for both sides, but especially for the Japanese, were governed by the reality of the caves. The Okinawa caves were in some ways a unique response to the lethal massed firepower of the enemy artillery the IJA 32nd Army faced and, given what they were intended to do, the caves were extremely successful.

Cave Warfare

The caves were largely responsible for the density and immobility of the fighting on Okinawa. Without them the Japanese would not have been able to continue to fight at all, and they greatly influenced the tactics both sides found themselves using. As an operational device, the Okinawa caves surpassed the trench systems of World War I in some respects, and in their self-sufficiency the caves were an evolutionary step toward the style of tunnel system used by the North Vietnamese at Cu Chi.

The Command Cave

The most elaborate of the caves was the headquarters structure for the IJA 32nd Army, far below Shuri Castle (see figures 1 and 2). The headquarters tunnel ran 425 yards north to south, with side chambers and a side shaft angling to the left at the north end. The 5th Artillery Command had its tunnel, about 200 yards long, just to the west. The 62nd Division headquarters cave lay 300 yards to the east.

The 32nd Army's command cave lay under sloping terrain, beneath 160 feet of earth at its deepest point, and beneath 50–100 feet for most of its length. The 32nd's command functions were all placed in 60 yards of the northwestern extremity of the tunnel's side shaft. The commanders were fortunate to be below Shuri Castle rather than in it because as the battle progressed its handsome buildings and parks were reduced to a mass of rubble.

Unlike the smaller front-line caves, the headquarters cave had all walls faced with sawed planks and supported with squared beams. Access shafts were provided with wooden ladders and landings every 12 feet or so. Climbing straight up 50–100 feet in these shafts was arduous. The furnishings were simple but useful, rather like an IJA barracks. Offices were set up with desks and chairs and had electricity. The commander's store was

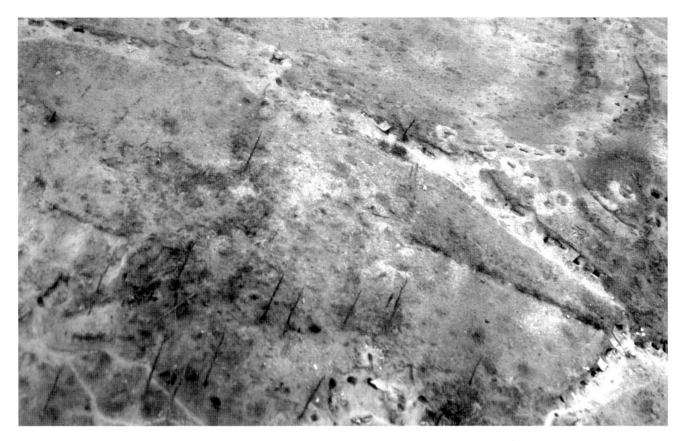

Above: Aerial of terrain near Love Hill north of Yonaburu. Thousands of Japanese troops frought from caves dug in the hillside.

Left: Soldiers of the US Tenth Army stand guard as one prepares to toss a hand grenade into the debris of an Okinawa tomb used by the Japanese as a pillbox. Dead Japanese lie in front of the tomb, which is constructed of concrete several inches thick.

notoriously well stocked, and 72 feet of tunnel at the south end served as the headquarters kitchen. Elaborate measures were taken to lead the smoke outlets to points where they would be screened from the Americans' view. In the soldiers' areas, bunks ran lengthwise along the side of the tunnel. The functions and spaces of the tunnels took on the quality of a warship.

As far as enemy fire was concerned, the Shuri command tunnel was completely safe. Life there, however, was not without its hardships. According to Yahara, the atmosphere was hot and humid, over 90 degrees Fahrenheit with 100 per cent humidity. Walls sweated and desks and chairs were sticky with moisture. The inhabitants developed skin rashes because their skin never dried. A large ventilator fan placed in one of the access shafts to bring in fresh air had a limited effect. Moreover, rice stored in the tunnels began to ferment in the sacks, giving it a sour taste

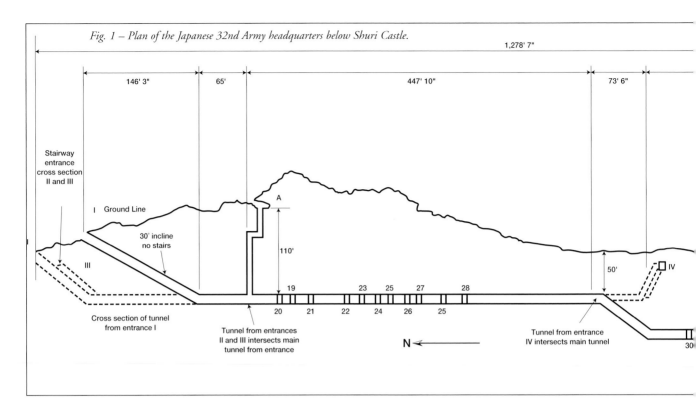

Fig. 1 – Plan of the Japanese 32nd Army headquarters below Shuri Castle.

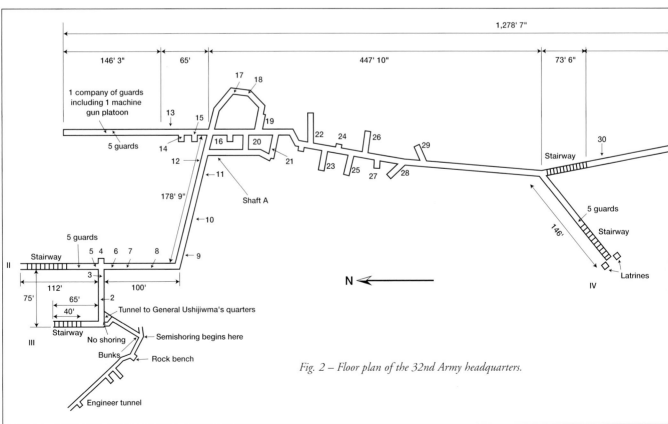

Fig. 2 – Floor plan of the 32nd Army headquarters.

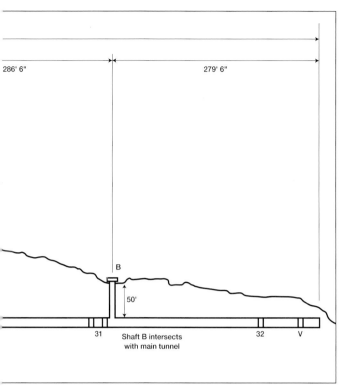

286' 6" 279' 6"

B

50'

31 Shaft B intersects 32 V
with main tunnel

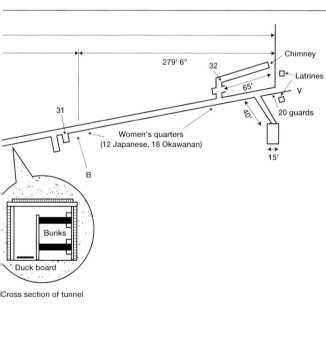

279' 6" 32 Chimney

□ Latrines

V

31 65'

40' 20 guards

Women's quarters
(12 Japanese, 18 Okawanan)

15'

B

Bunks

Duck board

Cross section of tunnel

Key to Fig. 1.

19	*Operations section, 24th Division*
20	*Commanding general's office and quarters, 24th Division*
21	*Staff office, 24th Division*
22	*Telegraph section, supply room*
23	*Intelligence section 44th IMB*
24	*First-aid station*
25	*Air intelligence section, 32nd Army*
26	*Dispensary*
27	*Staff officers' quarters*
28	*Construction section*
29	*Medical officers' office*
30	*Staff office, 44th IMB*
31	*Commanding officer (Rear Admiral Ota) and officers' quarters, Okinawa Naval Base Force, 10th–17th May 1945*
I-V	*Primary entrances*
A B	*Secondary entrances and ventilation shafts*

Key to Fig. 2.

1	*Commanding general's office and quarters*
2	*Chief of staff's office and quarters*
3	*Staff officers*
4	*Senior adjutant's office and quarters*
5	*Clerks and messengers*
6	*Operations office*
7	*Formerly commanding general's office and quarters 44th IMB, later quarters for 10 women typists*
8	*Commanding general's pantry*
9	*Telegraph section*
10	*Weather section*
11	*Material and personnel section*
12	*Reconnaissance section*
13	*Signal section*
14	*Telephone and switchboard*
15	*Officers' quarters*
16	*Order distributing centre*
17	*32nd Army intelligence section*
18	*Operations section, 24th Division*
19	*Operations section, 24th Division*
21	*Staff office, 24th Division*
22	*Telegraph section supply room, 32nd Army*
23	*Intelligence section, 44th IMB*
24	*First aid station*
25	*Air intelligence section*
26	*Dispensary*
27	*Staff officers' quarters*
28	*Construction section*
29	*Medical officers' office*
30	*Staff office, 44th IMB*
31	*Commanding officer (Rear Admiral Ota) and officers' quarters, Okinawa Naval Base Force 10th–17th May 1945*
32	*Kitchen*
A B	*Secondary entrances and ventilation shafts*
I–V	*Primary entrances*

Above: Trenches above Yontan airfield.

Right: Fig. 3 – Typical Japanese pillbox caves.

when served. Besides that, given the command staff, the sentries, the numerous messengers, and the headquarters company, there were over 1,000 troops in the tunnel. This made the air not only stuffy but also filled with human aromas. The press of people itself was a kind of hardship.

On the other hand, boosting morale, 30 intelligent young women (12 Japanese and 18 Okinawan) did office work in the cave and had their own living quarters at the cave's south end. There were also some creature comforts. Staples and canned goods were stored in considerable quantity, and pleasant meals were provided for the staff by the chef chief of staff Cho had brought from Fukuoka. Cho had also brought a pastry chef, who prepared the refreshments for afternoon tea. Fresh vegetables were harder to come by, but the sentries outside managed to forage some tomatoes and Chinese cabbage from neighbouring gardens. Beer and sake were plentiful, and the commander's store held respectable Scotch whiskies. Though cigarettes soon grew mouldy in the dampness of the cave, lucky staff members could occasionally get fresh Camels, as Yahara did, from American parachute supply drops that had carried into the Japanese lines.

Besides the physical rigours, there were psychological pressures that accompanied cave life. The headquarters cave was a 'nightless palace' where electric lights burned day and night, which was disorienting. Since messengers could move only at night, the battle situation could not begin to be pieced together until well after dark. Communication below battalion level was by messenger, communication at battalion level and above was by field telephone, but artillery bombardment often cut the telephone lines. Thus communication even at battalion level and above was often by messenger. The situation then had to be analysed, a response determined, and orders drafted. The result was to reverse night and day for the staff, who could not complete their work until just before dawn. Yahara wrote afterwards that he would fall asleep at dawn just as the American bombardment was beginning, with 'the feeling he was being dragged to the bottom of hell'. The strange life of the caves, even though shielded from battle, took its toll. Even the formidable Cho began mumbling in his sleep, 'Mother, it hurts.'

Line and Artillery Caves

Although the 32nd Army headquarters tunnel was the most imposing of the caves, there were many other underground structures, enough to house all 100,000 men of 32nd Army underground, 60 miles of tunnels in all. These caves were all located at the south end of Okinawa in an area 3–12 miles wide and 16 miles long; the whole battle area was honeycombed with defensive fortifications. Each company- and battalion-size unit was responsible for building its own tunnels. This seemed to guarantee that the job was done thoroughly but meant that there was considerable variety in the tunnel patterns. It also meant that fire nets were not well integrated for formations larger than battalions.

There was enough variety in the construction of the caves that one American officer described them as 'artful and fantastic'. Even so, what mainly varied was size, function, and the degree to which they were finished. The headquarters caves were the most elaborate. At the other extreme were the supply caves designed to hold ammunition and food. These differed from other tunnels in that they had wide mouths, wide shafts, and large chambers and did not have multiple openings. They were just modest underground storage rooms. One example of this type was found by Americans near the north end of the Okinawa isthmus. Somewhat akin to this style was the underground barracks room. This type featured long underground shafts with one or several entrances, a vertical air duct, a chamber 15 feet by 15 feet by 6 feet for eating, and another chamber for sleeping. Like the storerooms, these underground barracks were not fortifications.

Most of the honeycomb of tunnels the Japanese companies and battalions built for themselves, however, were underground fighting positions. Although these forts were made in a great variety of sizes and patterns, the principles they followed were all remarkably the same: they were pillboxes (see figure 3). The cave

LETHALITY IN MOTION: TACTICS

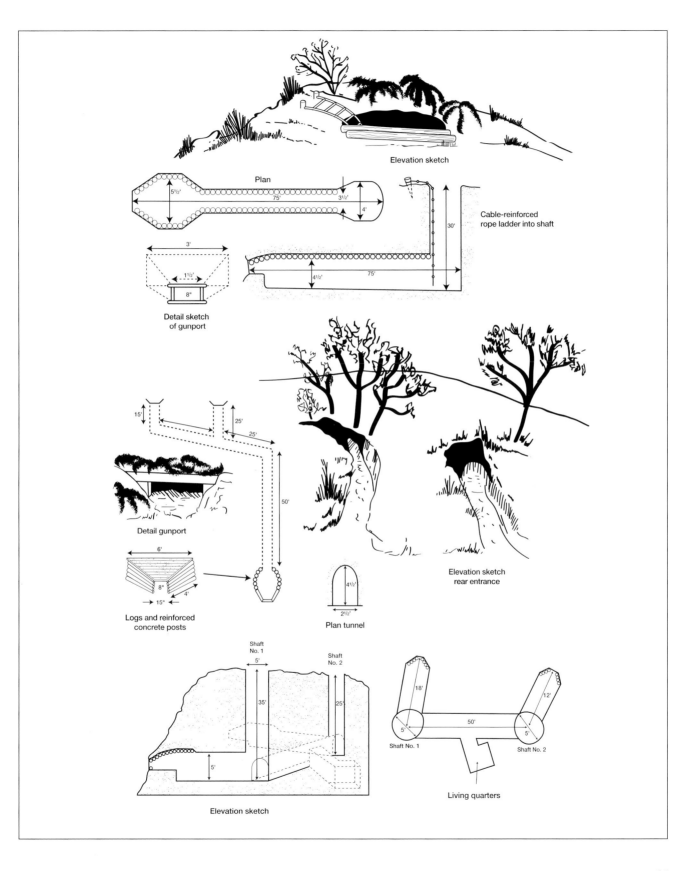

Elevation sketch

Plan

5½'   75'   3½'   4'

Cable-reinforced
rope ladder into shaft

30'

3'

1½'

8"

Detail sketch
of gunport

4½'   75'

Detail gunport

15'   25'   25'

50'

6'

8"   4'

15"

Logs and reinforced
concrete posts

4½'

2½'

Plan tunnel

Elevation sketch
rear entrance

Shaft
No. 1

Shaft
No. 2

5'

35'   25'

5'

Elevation sketch

18'   12'

50'

5'   5'

Shaft No. 1   Shaft No. 2

Living quarters

pillbox positions were in a sense not underground. Because of the undulating terrain and because the Japanese used only reverse-slope tactics, their technique was to dig horizontal shafts into the hill or ridge opposite the one they intended to cover with fire. Therefore, when they looked out of their fire ports, their perspective was one of a person at or above ground level. The caves' entrances were made by extending the cave shaft to the rear of the same hill whose front slope had the fire port. One entered the tunnel from the rear, without descending. These so-called caves might also be described as hilltop fortresses since they offered complete protection while also commanding the terrain. This may have kept the Japanese inhabitants' morale higher than that of their counterparts in World War I trenches or the caves of Cu Chi.

There was variety in the pillbox patterns due both to how many men were available in an area to construct a cave, and then garrison it, and what terrain features were available. Sometimes a whole round hilltop would be taken over with fire ports pierced out of every side and multiple concealed entrances on the side the enemy was least likely to approach. The air ventilation shaft would be extended vertically.

More often defenders found themselves on a continuous ridge that, unlike the round-topped hills, did not offer the possibility of side shafts, so shafts were cut straight back from the fire position. In the most elementary and most common of these, a shaft 4½ feet high and 3½ feet wide, as opposed to 5 feet by 6 feet in the deluxe Shuri headquarters cave, was pushed far back into the hillside, with a vertical entry shaft only if the back side of the hill was too far away. If there was a vertical entry shaft, it would have a simple rope and bamboo ladder, and its mouth would be covered by a wooden cover made like part of a traditional Japanese barrel and camouflaged with earth. The firing room was widened to perhaps 5½ feet, then tapered to the fire port. The port itself might be as small as 8 inches wide, with earth splayed outward from that opening to a width of 3 feet. This made it easy to fire out of and hard to fire into. Just inside the fire port would be a platform, a foot or so above the floor, on which was placed a machine gun or other weapon. All the construction in such a position consisted of shaped earth, with hand-cut logs to shore up the walls and the external splaying. The few men who manned the position usually lived inside in a slightly widened chamber or side shaft.

Since responsibility for building the caves lay with the battalions, communications between caves, like the fire nets between them, were well integrated at battalion level and below, but not above. Nearby caves were sometimes linked by tunnel. Caves farther apart were linked by communications trenches so soldiers could move between them unseen. The larger caves had

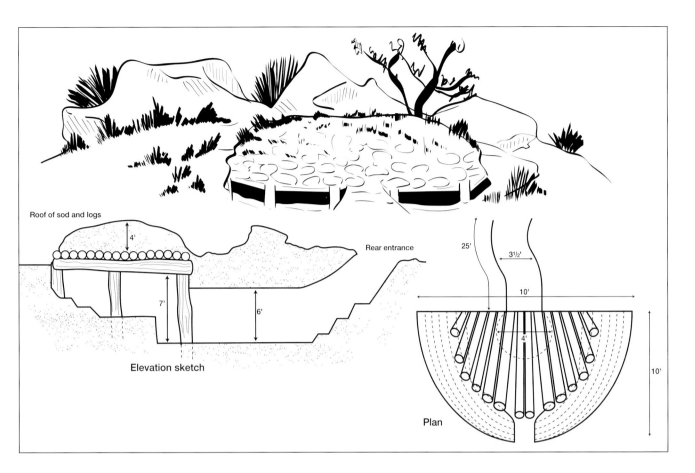

Roof of sod and logs

Rear entrance

Elevation sketch

Plan

Above: Fig. 5 – An IJA mortar position.

Left: Fig. 4 – An IJA 150mm naval gun position.

multiple entrances, and entrances in general, like the fire ports, were small and artfully concealed.

American observers came to believe that, in some of the larger hills, extensive tunnels provided underground mobility to the Japanese, and that this allowed them to convert an apparent defensive operation into an offensive one by moving troops through tunnels into different pillboxes. Some of the through-the-hill cave systems did indeed allow the Japanese free movement around a particular area without being seen.

The 32nd Army staff understood that being restricted to a cave system limited 32nd Army's mobility. Because the building of communications trenches had not been coordinated above battalion level, it was very difficult for large forces to manoeuvre out of sight. And if they did manage to move, there was often no room for them in the already crowded caves when they arrived. When preparing for attack, the problem could be overcome by painstakingly moving forces at night. But when responding to US attacks, which always came in the day, large forces could not be moved from one network of underground positions to another. Concentrating forces to resist an attack or mount a counter-attack was impossible.

This meant that Japanese soldiers in a position that was being attacked had to defend to the death, because their comrades could not come to their assistance, nor for that matter, could they retreat in the open without being exposed to massive American fire. The cave forts, although they protected the IJA force, sharply reduced its mobility, and manoeuvre was out of the question. This problem could have been partially overcome if the Japanese had paid more attention to building communications trenches between the scores of small cave systems.

American officers reported that the Japanese used the caves to manoeuvre behind the US lines. But it is more likely that the Japanese were trapped in their caves behind the Americans as a consequence of the Americans' forward movement. The cave positions prevented out-of-sight rearward mobility. Because the Japanese could not safely retreat, some ended up behind the American lines, though neither they nor the Americans wished for them to be there.

While the whole Japanese infantry was installed in pillbox caves, so was its artillery, both large and small pieces. Although the size of the cave varied according to the size of the gun, the configuration and function of the artillery caves were essentially the same as those of the infantry machine-gun caves. One of the two 150mm naval guns overlooking Nakagusuku (Buckner) Bay, for example, was set in a concrete-walled room 25 feet by 15 feet, with a reinforced concrete fire port 8 feet wide. The gun crew lived in a long shaft behind the firing room. In short the big-gun forts, like the machine-gun forts, were just fire slots with tunnel shelters behind them (see figure 4)

Searchlights and naval rangefinders were set next to a line-of-sight opening with a barracks tunnel behind, just as the guns were. In other words, the 'window-on-the-world' approach was adopted for all line-of-sight related functions. A semi-circular variation was provided for mortars. Typically, a 10-foot semicircular room was set 4 1/2 feet into the ground with a fan-shaped, hardened, camouflaged roof at ground level and an

Right: *Columns of smoke mark bomb hits on the town of Toguchi and a neighboring inlet during a US Navy carrier strike.*

Below: *Kadena airfield was extremely close to the shoreline.*

Below right: *The flat shoreline led on to a hillier interior.*

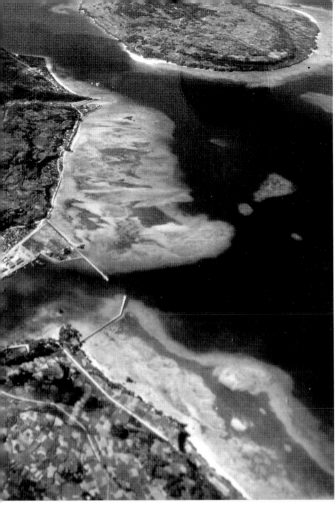

underground shaft running behind. Fire slots were created at intervals along the 180 degrees around the edge of the roof by removing some of the ground (see figure 5)

In many respects, the whole Okinawan struggle resembled a World War I battle in terms of the conditions the respective sides faced. Even so, the IJA cave systems had a personality different from the Western Front trench systems. The World War I trench systems did not put men continuously underground, nor were the major artillery pieces, rear headquarters, and rear area supply personnel underground. It was the American air presence that forced these combat support elements underground, because the American planes carried a weapon deadlier than guns or bombs: perfect knowledge of Japanese activities. Any activity that was seen would be blasted off the face of the earth by artillery fire.

There was another notable difference. Because of the undulating terrain, IJA units were able to build their forts into the hillsides while still giving a view on the world that was above ground level, and that seemed to and did dominate terrain. This, plus the fact that the caves were almost completely safe from bombardment, seems to have spared IJA soldiers some of the anxiety that World War I soldiers experienced living day in, day out, in the trenches. The Japanese soldiers did not suffer as much as the World War I soldiers from the 'underground neuroses' described by Eric Leed (see Bibliography). That the Americans never themselves went underground to engage in

World War I style mining and counter-mining, in effect underground manoeuvre combat, may also have saved the IJA soldier some mental stress.

Okinawa Terrain

The IJA 32nd Army chose to build its main defensive positions across the Okinawa isthmus near a line running from Uchitomari on the west coast to Tsuwa on the east (see map 3). The rugged terrain in this area, which extended southward to the Naha–Yonabaru line, was superbly fitted to the methods the IJA had adopted of using hilltop pillbox caves and reverse slope fields of fire that would force the Americans to attack with small teams of infantry soldiers. The terrain here was rolling and hilly and 'broken by terraces, steep natural escarpments, and ravines'. It was characterised by 'lack of pattern, steep slopes, and narrow valleys' and was 'filled with twisting ridges and spotted with irregular knolls'. Because the terrain was hilly and irregular, it provided innumerable short fields of fire but no long fields of fire. This was ideal for the Japanese whose defence relied on 'large numbers of short-range weapons'. The tangled, broken ground forced the Americans to fight a thousand small battles hand-to-hand instead of one large battle at a distance where their preponderant firepower would have given them the advantage.

Cave War Tactics

The IJA 32nd Army on Okinawa succeeded in doing what Robert E. Lee vowed, but failed, to do at Gettysburg: manoeuvre offensively but fight defensively. The 32nd Army placed itself where it knew the US Army must come, Okinawa, and it shrewdly chose terrain:

(1) that was strategically crucial for the Americans to capture for control of Nakagusuku Bay and Naha harbour,

yet which also

(2) was extremely favourable for the defender.

Having identified such terrain, the 32nd Army thoroughly prepared it. Creating the cave environment was itself the 32nd Army's greatest operational success.

The Japanese built the caves with fields of fire on reverse slopes and on important routes and integrated the cave fire nets, though not as well as they might have. Until US ground forces reached the hidden defence line across the southern isthmus, the 32nd Army stayed in its caves and did not respond to any air or sea reconnaissance efforts. The US Tenth Army therefore did not know where on Okinawa the IJA 32nd Army was. Reconnaissance aircraft could not identify IJA targets for the bombardment prior to landing. Even after landing, the Tenth Army was on the island

for eight days before it ran up against 32nd Army's main line of resistance at Kakazu and Minami-Uebaru.

Both the Japanese and the Americans had to accommodate themselves tactically to the existence of the caves. At first, the Americans did not know the pillbox caves even existed and had no doctrine for dealing with them. This was a severe disadvantage, but one for which the Americans on the front line soon found a solution. At the outset of the offensive the American forces advanced en masse and were mowed down in crowds by machine guns hidden in the caves when they reached the reverse slopes. American officers on the scene quickly developed a method to overcome this tactical problem. They would bombard the Japanese positions they faced, forcing the IJA off the surface. They would then infiltrate men in small numbers through narrow gaps in the Japanese fixed cave fire line ('dead ground'). The fact that the cave positions were separated and their fire nets not perfectly integrated then became a serious liability for the Japanese because the Americans took advantage of the small openings in the fire line to envelop the cave positions.

Developing and learning these tactics took time and explains the heavy losses suffered by each American division in the first two weeks of combat. Casualties for each American division's first two weeks of 'cave' fighting exceeded losses of subsequent weeks by 40 per cent or more (see Appendix). The only partial exception to this pattern was the 7th Infantry Division, which fought along the less densely defended eastern shoreline and which had had experience on Leyte of fighting in this type of terrain.

The Japanese counter-tactic to American ground infiltration was to leave more men on the surface during bombardment and to move more men out of their bunkers and back on the surface instantly when the bombardment stopped. These troops would attack the few Americans who had seeped through the gaps in the line and try, often successfully, to drive them back. The result was fierce small-arms fights between small units of men in isolated valleys not readily visible to either main force. These fights were usually fairly equal because the Americans had only

Above left: *Marines work over an LVT (A)-4. In the background the marshy beach stretches out to the distant tide.*

Left: *Fighting went on bitterly even after organized resistance on Okinawa ceased on 21st June. Here, M4s of 77th Infantry Division attempt to destroy a Japanese stronghold. The tank in the center has been knocked out and the others are protecting it and returning fire into the enemy position.*

Far left: *With Japanese shells bursting all around, American M4s move in on the enemy at Madeera.*

the light arms they could carry and could not use artillery at close quarters where they risked being hit by their own shell fire. Whenever the Americans were able they would ensure that their tanks were with their infantry, which was impossible for the Japanese. Losses in these small-arms fights were high. The Americans usually had to infiltrate their infantry forward several times before they could gain a foothold that was proof against the aggressive Japanese counter-attacks. The Japanese counter methods in some respects resembled the defensive tactics that evolved on the Western Front in World War I. Rather than attacking, the Japanese limited their efforts to counter-attacking and struck only against enemy elements which had precariously established themselves on the wrong side of the defence line. While the American attackers were still few and not dug in, a small IJA unit would charge firing their weapons and quickly drive the enemy out of their isolated strongpoint before they had time to consolidate their position. They had to do what storm troops were invented to do in World War I. Japanese artillery also concentrated their fire on the exposed positions of the Americans before they could dig in.

The fierce Japanese counter-attacks were notoriously effective, and indeed it was here that the IJA's orthodox doctrine emphasising bold and hasty attack served 32nd Army well. The quick death-defying attacks by a platoon or a company, armed only with bolt-action rifles and knee mortars, was something IJA training had prepared 32nd Army for well, even though that same training was inappropriate for all the rest of the Okinawa experience.

Tanks Versus Caves

Use of unaccompanied infantry in attacks against cave positions was not very successful, and if this had been the Americans' only resource, their progress could have been halted. Indeed there could have been a stalemate on Okinawa despite the Americans' firepower, in which both sides dug in and neither side could move. What made it possible for the Americans to advance expeditiously against the IJA's ingenious caves was the tank. The tank did not make it easy to move through the densely entrenched fire-swept zone, but it made it possible. The tanks provided the Americans with an answer to the caves in this kind of warfare. Tanks protected by infantry were able to deal with the gun-port caves, which were also protected by infantry.

In other words the basic tactical unit on each side was a pillbox and accompanying infantry. The Americans used a mobile, somewhat vulnerable pillbox, the tank, against the Japanese who used almost invulnerable but not mobile pillboxes,

Above and Below: *These tanks were knocked out by Japanese mines.*

Right: *Close-up of a large Japanese mine used against American troops on Okinawa.*

the caves. To a certain extent the Japanese overcame the immobility of the cave pillboxes by having caves everywhere and moving among them. As in World War I, much of the combat, despite the massive artillery activity, came to involve infantry fighting around machine-gun strongpoints, only on the American side the strongpoints themselves were moving. In the end, these actions came down to small-arms and mortar fights at company and platoon levels, and sometimes included hand-to-hand combat.

Japanese Anti-tank Tactics

Even though Japanese anti-tank tactics were systematic, they were ultimately ineffective. Their failure, however, was not due to the Japanese lack of information about American tanks. The 32nd Army had anticipated the pivotal role of tanks on Okinawa: 'fighting against the American land army is practically the same thing as fighting against M4 tanks', 32nd Army Directive No. 13 intoned.

The Japanese forces were advised to wait until the American tanks were very close to their positions and then to open fire both on the tank with artillery and on the accompanying infantry with small arms and mortars. The Japanese anti-tank weapons included the 37mm gun, which had a limited effect on the Sherman tank, and also the 47mm anti-tank gun, which was effective. The 47mm gun, designed in 1941 as a modern anti-tank weapon, had been distributed in limited numbers to Japanese 32nd Army forces. It had a muzzle velocity of 2,700 feet per second, had rubber tyres, and weighed 1,600 pounds, which meant it could theoretically be manhandled, though in fact the 47mm guns were usually placed in cave pillboxes where they were not mobile.

Even though the 47mm gun would 'perforate any armour of the M4A6 tank at all ranges up to 800 yards', the Japanese doctrine in all cases was to withhold fire until the enemy's tank team was quite close. This ensured that the Japanese position was saved longer from discovery and gave the 47mm gun a surer shot. If no gun was available, the enemy tank, if allowed to approach unopposed, would be nearer to anti-tank infantry.

Once the enemy tanks approached, IJA soldiers would unleash small-arms, mortar, and anti-tank artillery fire all at once to destroy both the tank and the infantry team. If no 47mm guns were on hand or if the gun failed to destroy the tank, the IJA soldiers' next tactic was to drive the US infantry away from the tank using small arms and mortars. This left the tanks 'blind', as a Japanese tactical bulletin put it. The Japanese also attempted to kill the commander of an American tank if he was standing in the hatch.

Captain Ito Koichi of the 24th Division maintained that American Sherman tanks withdrew if they were fired on by light mortars, even though the mortars would not harm a Sherman. The reason, he believed, was that the American tank crew could not distinguish the mortar shell explosions from more dangerous howitzer shell explosions. In reality, Captain Ito may have been witnessing the American tanks' efforts to stay with their infantry when the latter fell back to avoid mortar bombardment.

Tanks that did not stay with their infantry were exposed to the IJA's third tactical step, which was to destroy the tank with hand-carried explosives – satchel charges, reinforced grenades, and mines. Most of these devices were powerful enough to damage a tread or the bogie wheels of a tank, thereby immobilising it, but they were not powerful enough to breach

the hull. The attackers tried to remain concealed until the first volley of small-arms fire had driven off American infantry, then they assaulted the tank. Often, the tanks' likely avenues of approach were mined so that the advancing tank might be immobilised in this way.

Immobilised tanks continued to be a main focus of struggle for the Japanese. Captain Ito claims that the most effective method of attack for lightly armed men against tanks was to immobilise the tank with a satchel charge or mine, then destroy it at leisure with Molotov cocktails. In fact American crews hastily abandoned such immobilised tanks, hoping to recover them after nightfall. Therefore Japanese engineers were advised to move in and blow up immobilised tanks before nightfall. Sometimes the Japanese were content just to place mines around

Above and Left: *Flamethrowers were an important part of anti-cave tactics. Not widely available at the start of the Pacific war, the M1 was first deployed on Guadalcanal at the beginning of 1943. It was very limited in range (around 50 feet) and so other versions were developed – the M1A1 effective to 150 feet and M2-2 to 200 feet.*

Far left: *Machine gun troops of the 77th Infantry Division advance in single file carrying the guns and their tripods.*

the damaged vehicle, especially on the probable route down which the tank would be towed away. Japanese soldiers often laid mines at night in tracks made by the treads, expecting the American tanks to use the same route again. This gave IJA infantry a chance to ambush the party who were planning to recover the damaged tank.

Japanese anti-tank tactics, in sum, involved:

(1) destroying the tank with an anti-tank gun,

(2) driving off its supporting infantry with small arms and destroying the tank with hand-carried explosives, or

(3) immobilising the tank and destroying it later.

Conspicuously absent from their anti-tank system were bazooka-type infantry anti-tank weapons. The Japanese had

Above: *Sherman flamethrower of the 32nd Regiment of the 77th Infantry Division in action against a Japanese cave on Hill 95.*

Right: *US troops advance inland. Note flamethrower third from rear.*

Far right: *US infantrymen of the Tenth Army advance behind a tank in a wooded area shortly after landings.*

received some information on the Panzerfaust anti-tank weapon from the Germans but had not used this to produce examples for service. Very seldom was heavy artillery used in an anti-tank roles. The IJA had the artillery but did not have radio contact between the small line units in the front and the artillery in the rear that would have made attack on particular tanks possible. The lack of bazookas and radios, and the also the relative dearth of 47mm anti-tank guns, was extremely serious. The liberal presence of these items could have slowed the advance of the American tanks significantly and prolonged the Okinawa stalemate.

This Japanese failure to provide bazookas and radios was all the more serious because the modest technology and resources needed for both were available. If some of the resources devoted to well-machined field guns, howitzers, and mortars on Okinawa had been devoted instead to some humbler anti-tank weapons, the battlefield might have been transformed. The inadequacy of IJA field equipment must be attributed in the end to doctrinal prejudice. Somehow, the IJA's conceptual approach to combat did

not include or anticipate an armoured adversary or an environment where a company's only possible link to the larger battlefield was by radio. These shortcomings are the more blameworthy since the IJA had had similar problems with the Russians at Nomonhan in 1939 but had done nothing about them.

American Anti-Cave Tactics

American tactics for destroying caves resembled Japanese tactics for destroying tanks. The Americans used artillery, flamethrowers, and small arms to drive in the caves' protective infantry, thus allowing friendly infantry to approach the cave and disable it so the whole cave position could then be destroyed at leisure. The result in practice was that, between bombardments, there were lethal firefights between small units of infantry to see which infantry could reach the other's hardened pillboxes, tanks, and caves.

The cave positions on Okinawa were a defensive masterpiece, impervious to all fire, except a direct hit on the gun-port. This gave the IJA soldiers a false sense of security, however, and in the early days of battle produced false tactics. Defenders found that, despite the caves' strength against fire, they could easily be breached if surrounded by infantry. The caves had a limited field of vision, like tanks, so their occupants did not even know where attackers were.

To protect infantry from the crushing American bombardments, IJA companies were advised to withdraw all their men into the caves, except for two or three sentries. But the unhappy result of this was that, when the bombardments ceased, American tank–infantry teams rushed forward to seize cave entrances, thus trapping whole companies and their weapons helplessly inside. Holding all IJA infantry safe in the caves was therefore not as prudent for the Japanese as it first appeared.

The Japanese response was to leave ten or twelve men per company outside, even during heavy bombardment. Their job was to survive the bombardment, then hold off the advancing American infantry long enough for their comrades to emerge from the cave to help hold the ground. The mature cave positions thus had interlocking fire and were screened by a system of foxholes that were manned at all times (see figure 4). There was not enough room between the caves to deploy the entire force under cover outside, however, so only one-third of the troops would be put outside when the bombardment stopped. This meant that the two-thirds of the troops remaining in the cave always risked being trapped helplessly underground.

The American method for reducing the caves, which they called 'blowtorch and corkscrew' and the Japanese called 'cavalry charge', was to bombard the cave area, killing surface infantry or forcing them inside. This alone did not subdue the cave-protected infantry, so the Americans then approached with tanks and infantry teams. These together drove the remaining IJA infantry away from the cave entrances.

Fire from the tanks' machine guns, main guns, or flamethrowers was used to push IJA gunners away from the cave fire ports long enough for US infantry to get past their angles of fire into what the Japanese called the 'dead angle'. Actually, to increase firepower, the IJA often had riflemen fire at angles off the machine gun or cannon in the fire port. They called this 'sleeve' tactics. In order to get into the dead spaces, the Americans had first to break through the Japanese infantry defence line. Once they had done that, though, the cave positions were completely helpless. The Japanese called this a 'straddle' attack since American riflemen straddled the exits with their fire instead of standing directly in front of the exit openings where IJA soldiers could fire on them. The Americans could not fire in from these positions either, but they could shoot any Japanese trying to exit.

Many of the caves were situated under the dome of a hill, with exits on the sides and the rear of the dome, and a fire port facing the front. The Japanese especially dreaded the Americans' advance to the top of the dome. The summit was outside the fire port's fire angle and often covered every exit, so that one American standing there with a machine gun could prevent all escapes from the cave, despite its multiple exits. Even if no dome existed, the American infantry would sweep to the far side of the hill where the cave was and cover the rear slope exits so that inmates had no choice but to surrender. Usually the Americans tried to find the air shaft above a cave and throw in a phosphorus grenade, a smoke bomb, or other explosives. Sometimes, they would pump in large amounts of petrol, which they then ignited. These methods either killed the soldiers inside or forced them out. Having done this, the Americans either sealed the cave by blowing up the exits or occasionally entered it to take possession. With this, the caves were considered secure, and the Americans moved forward.

Where caves were only haphazardly subdued, the IJA soldiers stationed inside continued to resist. The Americans' task was to seal every exit before nightfall. Often, however, they failed to find all the exits, or else they blew up an exit in a way that widened the opening rather than blocking it. In either case, the Japanese would escape from the exits after dark and engage in rear-area attacks or return to their own lines. On the other hand, there were a few Japanese soldiers who stayed quietly in their caves for months after they had been bypassed and surrendered only when Japan did, some time after the campaign in Okinawa had been concluded.

In the tank-versus-cave warfare, a moving strongpoint – the tank – was pitted against a fixed strongpoint – the cave – with infantry manoeuvring to protect each.

Japanese Artillery

Although the Americans had firepower which greatly exceeded that of the Japanese in all categories, the Japanese 32nd Army nevertheless had considerable artillery on Okinawa. The Japanese forces had confidence in their artillery, though the American experts who examined it after the battle were critical of certain features. To unify control over the artillery, it was all gathered into 32nd Army's 5th Artillery Command, under

Lieutenant-General Wada Kosuke. This included three artillery regiments, an artillery battalion, a mortar regiment, and two light mortar battalions. Besides these there were the 24th Division's artillery regiment and the 44th IMB's artillery battalion, both also placed under Wada's direction.

All of these units together held 287 guns and 30 mortars of 70mm bore or more for a total of 317 tubes, according to the count of US Tenth Army intelligence after the battle. Inagaki Takeshi, a Japanese journalist who has investigated the Okinawa campaign, gives a figure of 470 tubes for 32nd Army, a tally that apparently includes guns of smaller calibre. Inagaki notes that, when the front had been reduced to the five-mile width of the Shuri isthmus, this was the heaviest concentration of Japanese guns in any Pacific battle.

Although there were a few 200mm naval guns, most of the guns were either 75mm or 150mm. The 1st Artillery Mortar Regiment also used 24 x 320mm spigot mortars. These mortars, which had a range of three-quarters of a mile, fired shells that weighed 650 pounds and left a crater 15 feet wide and 8 feet deep. The Japanese staff officers believed, and with some justification, that these shells frightened the Americans. Even so, these amazing weapons produced few casualties, because they had a 'terrific blast effect but practically no fragmentation'. Men quite close to the 15-foot crater were unharmed.

The 32nd Army's artillery, like its other branches, was constantly governed by the reality of American bombardment. Almost all the field guns were put in cave mouths, just like the machine guns and anti-tank guns. The difference was that the artillery caves were larger and located in the interior of the Okinawa land mass, away from the battle line. The guns were rolled to the narrow fire port when in use and away from it when not. Some guns had steel rails or wooden planks on the cave floor to facilitate this. The gun crews lived in the rear of the caves of the guns they served.

A few rear-area guns were left in the open, and some Japanese crews preferred this because they believed casualties were less in the case of American counter-fire. Crews caught in a bombarded cave mouth could not disperse and suffered heavy losses, even though the guns themselves were often dug out and reused after a direct hit. All anti-aircraft guns obviously had to be left in the open to preserve their field of fire, but they were then carefully camouflaged. For more protection, crews fashioned dummy guns and carriages of logs, and these guns were also carefully camouflaged. For American airmen, it was very difficult to tell the difference between the camouflaged real anti-aircraft guns and the camouflaged wooden ones.

The effect of all this artillery was nonetheless limited. The 5th Artillery Command was largely hamstrung by the weakness of its communications system. Japanese artillery relied on field telephones to transmit fire requests. This was the case between

*Below left and Below: Examples of Japanese artillery – US Marines examine a captured Japanese six-inch gun (**Below left**); an officer of the Chinese Expeditionary Force stands beside a Japanese Type 91 105mm artillery piece (**Below**). The emplacement was knocked out by flamethrowers and artillery.*

regimental observation posts of the 1st Medium Artillery Regiment and its gun emplacements, for example, in whose position, although the distances were not great, wires were left exposed and were not well distributed among different routes.

Wire was also used between infantry battalion headquarters, where fire requests originated, and the 5th Artillery Command in the rear. Units smaller than battalion had no communication system except messengers. These wires were frequently cut by American bombardment during the day, forcing infantry needing artillery to rely on coded radio messages or on runners. Radio transmission in code was slow, and reception was often impossible when senders or receivers were deep in the caves. Runners were extremely slow. The consequence was that an artillery request normally took six hours to fulfil. Therefore there was virtually no close infantry support by the field artillery. There were general bombardments preparatory to the Japanese offensives of 12th April and 4th May, however.

Japanese gunners customarily fired only a few rounds and then pulled the guns away from the cave mouths. They did this to avoid drawing devastating American counter-fire. American forces used new GR-6 sound locator devices to find the Japanese guns. Americans called the short firing time 'sniping', which frustrated their efforts to get a bearing. When the Americans got a bearing, they would blanket the area with fire or else send in a Cub reconnaissance plane to pinpoint the offending gun and try for a direct hit. The Japanese tried to ward off the Cubs with anti-aircraft fire or obstruct their observation with smoke, but were not always successful.

The Japanese ordinarily fired at dusk, night, or dawn, also to minimise counter-fire. Sometimes they fired spotter rounds at dusk so they would be on target during the night. Most of the Japanese fire, however, was 'prearranged fire delivered by uncorrected map data'. Most of the Japanese targets were unobserved and unobservable. Artillery battalions sometimes sent liaison officers to the infantry regiments they were supporting, but these officers were not forward observers, and indeed, the Japanese 5th Artillery Command did not have any forward observers with the infantry. Sometimes a few artillery personnel and an officer would infiltrate American lines at night to bring back map coordinates for suitable targets, but these fires also were then delivered by uncorrected map data.

The Japanese never massed their battery fires except for a major offensive, and they were criticised by the Americans for this. There were good reasons why the Japanese did not mass fires, however. Not only did massed fires draw counter-fire, they wasted the limited ammunition supply. The 5th Artillery Command had only 1,000 rounds per gun; therefore, saturation

fire was out of the question. Lieutenant-General Wada had imposed a reasonable working maximum of 50 shells per day per gun. Besides that, radio and visual communication between guns was limited by their physical isolation underground so that fire coordination would have been difficult in any case.

All in all, Japanese use of artillery was efficiently parsimonious. It was nevertheless flawed by lack of responsiveness to particular needs on the front line, a shortcoming that could have been

Above: This is the most successful Japanese infantry gun – the 70mm Type 92 Battalion Gun.

largely overcome, despite cave emplacement, with a more effective communications system. The front line infantry needed radios below the battalion level, and the artillery men, in their caves, needed antennas to receive their messages. To rely on runners moving several miles in the open to relay fire requests or fire observation meant that hitting targets of opportunity was out of the question. The 5th Artillery Command gunners were given credit for thorough use of pre-registered fires. In the event that

was all they were able to achieve. The Japanese amassed a large artillery force on Okinawa, but because of limited ammunition and communications, and forced segregation underground, sniping was the most it could do.

CHAPTER 4 Attack and Retreat, May 1945

The fighting on the Shuri line took the form of tanks-versus-caves for much of the Okinawa campaign. The tactical situation suddenly changed on the morning of 4th May, when the 32nd Army left its caves to launch a major assault on US lines. The Japanese decision to leave the comparative safety of their cave fortifications for the attack was then, and still is, controversial. Both the issues and the personalities surrounding the 4th May offensive were similar to those of the modest 12th April offensive. However, pressure from IGHQ and 10th Area Army, a crucial element in the 12th April decision, was absent this time. Instead, chief of staff Cho and the operations officer Yahara clashed over what for 32nd Army was a perpetual dilemma of doctrine.

On 22nd April, the 24th Division and the 44th IMB had been moved north to support the deteriorating position of the 62nd Division, relieving its right flank and forming a second line in its left rear respectively. Colonel Yahara, having at last resolved the north versus south problem and formed a strong defensive line, was content with the situation. The 32nd Army was implementing the kind of solid defence by attrition Yahara had envisioned from the start. Despite their 10-to-1 advantage in firepower and 2-to-1 advantage in manpower, the Americans' advance was being held to a modest 100 yards per day. Moreover, by the end of April, the 32nd Army had become the only Japanese force to have maintained organised resistance to an American island landing for over 30 days.

Yahara's optimism about 32nd Army's achievements was shared only by a minority of the 32nd Army staff. Most of the other members suffered from a growing feeling of pessimism, which in turn fuelled a growing desire for a bold attack that might break the status quo. Unlike Yahara, who thought they were doing well with what they had, other members of the staff were preoccupied with presentiment of total failure. Inexorably

the 32nd Army was being pushed back, and the eventual result of the tactics now being used would be that all of them would perish and Okinawa would be lost. The sombre mood of the staff was aggravated by conditions in the headquarters cave. American lines were getting closer, and the enemy shells continuously fell around its entrances. Every day the sentries posted at the entrances were being killed. Smoke from exploding shells was regularly sucked into the ventilator shaft, which would then precipitate one of the soldiers to shout a warning 'gas attack' sending the staff and all the other personnel scurrying around looking for their for gas masks. The stress of the situation, especially the realisation that death was inevitable, was beginning to take its toll on everyone.

The 29th April Meeting

In this environment, Lieutenant-General Cho called a staff meeting on 29th April to discuss operations. Cho spoke strongly in favour of an offensive. He had made up his mind well before the meeting since he had on 27th April asked Major Jin, the aviation staff member, to begin research on a possible attack. Cho argued that in the present state of affairs, the Americans had the upper hand. If the status quo continued, the 32nd Army would inevitably be wiped out. The solution was to use their surplus resources for an offensive while they still could. In this way, they might break out of the current deadlock and avoid certain defeat.

At this meeting, only Yahara spoke for continuing the war of attrition and avoiding an offensive. Yahara pointed out that in modern warfare a superiority of 3-to-1 was usually needed for successful attack. 'To take the offensive with inferior forces is reckless and would lead to certain defeat', he said. Second, the high ground around Minami-Uebaru had already fallen into American hands, giving them a major advantage in defensive

Braving Japanese sniper fire, US Marine Lieutenant Colonel R. P. Ross, Jr., places the American flag on a parapet of Shuri Castle on 29th May 1945.

Above: *A Marine of the 1st Marine Division using a Thompson sub-machine gun on Wana Ridge near Shuri.*

Above right: *A Tenth Army 155mm artillery battery pounds enemy positions.*

terrain. Third, Yahara argued, a hasty offensive would fail, with thousands needlessly lost. Then, 32nd Army's reduced forces would be unable to hold Okinawa for a long period and unable to delay the US invasion of Japan. A hasty attack would cause 32nd Army to fail in its duty.

Major Jin then spoke. Jin had favoured greater efforts to protect the Yontan and Kadena airfields from the start. Jin, like Cho, described the need for an offensive and its possible success. The other young staff members were silent. Cho then declared again that he hoped for an attack to snatch life from the midst of death. At this, Yahara left the room. All the other staff members then agreed to launch an offensive.

The 29th April staff meeting was as bitterly argued as the two earlier strategy meetings on 3rd and 10th April had been. Like the April meetings, it did not settle the issue for Yahara. He continued to oppose an offensive, and Cho continued to favour one. Cho then tried this time to manage Yahara by sheer emotional force. At dawn on 30th April, before Yahara 'had time to splash water on his face', Cho appeared at his quarters. Cho squeezed Yahara's hand and said with genuine enthusiasm that there had been nothing but trouble between them in the past and that they would probably both die together on Okinawa.

Cho then asked if Yahara, on this one occasion, would go along with the offensive. As Cho spoke, his tears fell abundantly. Yahara was deeply moved, despite his aloof reputation, and before long he was weeping too. He was overcome by Cho's sudden display of emotion and said, 'I consent.'

Lest this display of emotional pressure still not be enough, Lieutenant-General Ushijima, commander of 32nd Army, took Yahara aside in the staff office the same day and sternly advised him not to undermine support for the attack. Mild-mannered Ushijima never spoke to anyone in this way, and Yahara understood that Cho was also behind this rebuke. Yahara said he thought the offensive was a meaningless suicide attack but that he would support it since it was decided. Ushijima replied quietly that, of course, the offensive would be an honourable death attack.

Even Yahara went along with the attack plans by the end of April, in public at least. There were a number of reasons why an immediate offensive was decided on even though its military use was doubtful. One of these was Cho's forceful personality, which sometimes simply overwhelmed those about him. Another was that the received doctrine of the IJA for many years had been to secure quick victory by attack, especially a flank attack followed by hand-to-hand fighting. Cadets at the JMA were taught that one Japanese division with a robust spirit of attack could defeat three Soviet divisions with superior equipment. Officers raised in this tradition had an exaggerated faith in the effectiveness of attack. The impact of this training no doubt contributed to 32nd Army's decision for an offensive.

A third reason for the 32nd Army's decision to attack was the spirit of gloom surrounding the staff. The staff's feeling of frustration at their resources being worn down by the American advance caused them all to welcome a gamble, even with such long odds, that would at least give them hope. The attack would provide psychological relief from the stress of continuous defeat. Unfortunately, this was relief for the 32nd Army staff only. The 62nd Division, continuously in action, suffered stresses worse than the psychological kind and, in any case, was not to take part in the offensive. The 24th Division, which was nominated to carry out the attacks, had felt no such stress because it had not yet been exposed to combat. On this point, the 32nd Army staff may be criticised. Its mounting of a major offensive to relieve its own psychological discomfort was unprofessional.

Honourable Death Attack and Ritual Suicide

After the 29th April staff conference, Ushijima spoke for the first time in terms of an 'honourable death attack'. Honourable death (gyokusai) and ritual disembowelment (seppuku or hara-kiri), self-destruction for units and individuals respectively, were a powerful part of Japanese military culture. Honourable death, literally 'smashing the [imperial] jewel', meant that a unit fought until its last member died in combat, refusing to flee or surrender. Every school child was taught famous historical instances of the phenomenon. The concept probably evolved out of the conditions of Japan's Warring States period (1470–1600), when whole units sometimes fled or changed sides, but where the samurai closest to their feudal masters were

expected to fight to the death and where soldiers were normally tortured and killed if taken alive. The Japanese may have felt more threatened than other societies by the possibility that the ordinary soldier would flee from battle and therefore had strong inhibitions against flight. Being captured also raised a suspicion of disloyalty and selfish desire for self-preservation. The samurai or officer who quit fighting to surrender put his personal desires ahead of his cause, which in turn showed a deeply flawed character. Related to this was the traditional treatment of prisoners of war, which was that they were either killed, tortured and killed, or incarcerated with so few amenities that they soon died in captivity. That prisoners were worthy of respect and might be exchanged was an idea that did not exist in the Japanese mind. Rather, the Japanese believed absolutely that for a unit to perish in combat was very honourable.

The notion of individual suicide for soldiers derived from similar considerations. The samurai or officer in danger of being captured alive was expected to take his own life, according to proper ritual forms if possible. If 'honourable death attacks' failed, officers and, in the 1940s, private soldiers as well, were obliged to commit suicide. This showed sincerity, avoided harsh captivity, and prevented the enemy from using captives to manipulate those who had still not been captured. The tradition of suicide also may have relieved psychological stress, paradoxically, because its suffering was brief, self-administered, and held no loss of dignity, and because the soldier entering combat knew from the outset that nothing worse than that need happen to him. Suicide to avoid capture also helped guarantee normal military benefits for the victim's surviving family.

The staff of the 32nd Army thought increasingly in terms of honourable death attack and suicide in the latter part of the Okinawa campaign. Honourable death and ritual suicide held not only a practical military appeal but also a romantic appeal because of popular cultural traditions. Yahara opposed premature resort to honourable death, however, and often said so. He felt it was self-indulgent to make operational decisions because of romantic sentiment toward suicide and equally self-indulgent to seek an early and glorious escape instead of facing the heavy operational burdens still at hand.

Preparing the 4th May Offensive

Once the commanders had agreed on an offensive and formally set it for 4th May, it was up to Yahara to draft the plans with the help of staff members Majors Nagano and Kusumaru. Yahara performed this task diligently but still had not abandoned his wish to minimise the ill effects of the offensive, and so he inserted a minor change likely to have a major consequence. The ambitious

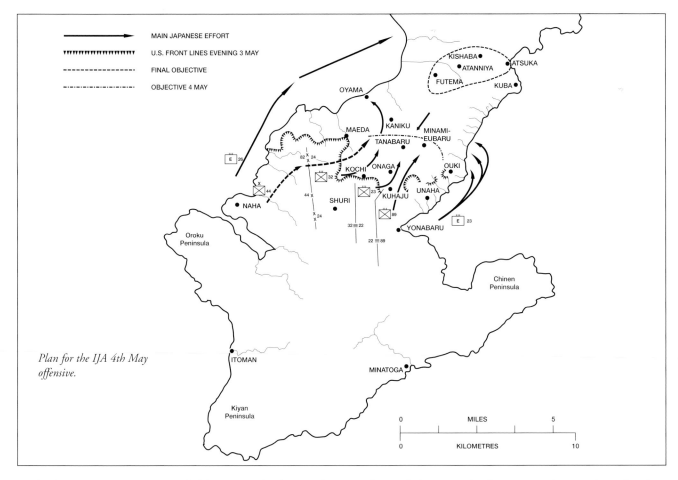

LEGEND:
- → MAIN JAPANESE EFFORT
- ▼▼▼▼▼▼▼▼▼▼▼▼▼▼ U.S. FRONT LINES EVENING 3 MAY
- - - - - - - FINAL OBJECTIVE
- -·- -·- -·- OBJECTIVE 4 MAY

Plan for the IJA 4th May offensive.

battle plan, in eight sections, provided for counter-landings in the American rear by the 23rd and 26th Shipping Engineer Regiments on the east and west coasts respectively (see map 7). The 62nd Division, holding the left half of the Japanese line, was to maintain its position, then go on the offensive once attacking units on its right had broken through. The 24th Division was to provide the main weight of the offensive and punch through on the right half of the line. The preparatory barrage was to begin at 00:45, on 4th May, and last for 30 minutes. The 24th Division was then expected to sweep past the Tanabaru escarpment to the Minami-Uebaru hill and eventually reach Futema.

On 3rd May the 44th IMB was to move from its reserve line behind the 62nd Division to a position northeast of Shuri. On 4th May when the 24th Division moved forward, the 44th IMB was to drive northwest through the opening to the coast town of Oyama, thus cutting off the US 1st Marine Division from retreat. Also, the IJN's infantry force was to put together four elite battalions and hold them in readiness, and the commander of 32nd Army, as the lines moved forward, was to transfer his headquarters to Maeda.

The small, but critical, adjustment Yahara made in the plans was that he would have had the 44th IMB move on 4th May, not 3rd May. This change of date meant that 44th IMB would not be on hand in time to participate in the attack, thus reducing the attack force by a third. Yahara's objective was, in fact, to keep 44th IMB out of the battle and thereby reduce casualties. Cho spotted the change in the first draft of the plans, however, and required Yahara to restore the original date. Yahara has earned both sympathy and criticism for altering the 44th IMB's movement date. He was doing what he thought was in the best interests of the army. But he was also personally subverting duly promulgated orders on which his superiors and the rest of the staff had agreed. Even though later events proved Yahara's judgment to be right, commentators have pointed to the impropriety of his conduct.

Once the plans had been set and preparations were suitably under way, Ushijima and Cho held a pre-victory banquet in their rooms of the headquarters cave. The only guests were the nine general officers. Electric lights blazed, and food and drink were plentiful. Cho's skilled chef prepared a feast from the supply of canned goods. Fine Scotch came out of Ushijima's store. The headquarters office girls came dressed attractively to serve the food and pour the drinks, and there was much gaiety and laughter. Ushijima and the rest, in high spirits, congratulated each other on the next day's victories of which they were so confident. Yahara was reminded of Wellington's ball before Waterloo, and other officers aware of the ball perhaps were too.

Results of the 4th May Offensive

Even as Ushijima's banquet was taking place, offensive operations had begun. The 26th and 23rd Shipping Engineer Regiments set out up the west and east coasts. Also, small groups of soldiers with light machine guns infiltrated behind US lines on the night of 3rd May to attack Americans as they became visible at dawn.

The main attack by the 24th Division began as planned. The artillery opened at 00:45, 4th May, and 24th Division's advance began soon after. By 00:53, 89th Regiment had penetrated the sector northeast of Onaga village and attacked on the right toward Unaha (see map 8). The 32nd Regiment on the left was to follow and capture the hill touching Maeda village's east end and then move forward to take the Tanabaru escarpment. The 22nd Regiment in the 24th Division's centre was to go forward and lay smoke, then attack toward Onaga, joining itself to the left flank of the 89th Regiment.

On the morning of 4th May, all of this seemed to go forward splendidly. The staff officers of 32nd Army, including Yahara, were all smiles and congratulations. Ushijima joked that perhaps it was now time to move his headquarters forward to Maeda. After noon, realistic battle reports began to come in from the front-line, and spirits were again dampened. Adding to this effect was the fact that the Japanese artillery fire that had dominated in the morning no longer did so, and instead a heavy American counter-bombardment had begun.

The 89th Regiment on the far right had moved forward a few thousand yards before being blocked by the US 7th Infantry Division. As it was now fighting in the open, the 89th Regiment was suffering heavy casualties, caused by concentrated land, naval, and air bombardment; it lost half its strength. The 22nd Regiment in the centre had even less luck, its advance being delayed by its task of laying smoke, and it suffered especially when the smoke unexpectedly cleared. American sources say the attacks were contained by 08:00 on 4th May, and Japanese sources indicate that forward movement on the right had ceased by 12:00.

On the left flank of the 24th Division's line, the 32nd Regiment was supposed to capture Maeda hill, then sweep forward and secure the Tanabaru escarpment. The 32nd, however, became entangled with the rightmost elements of the 62nd Division, causing confused fighting in the vicinity of Maeda hill to become more so, and the attack on Maeda failed.

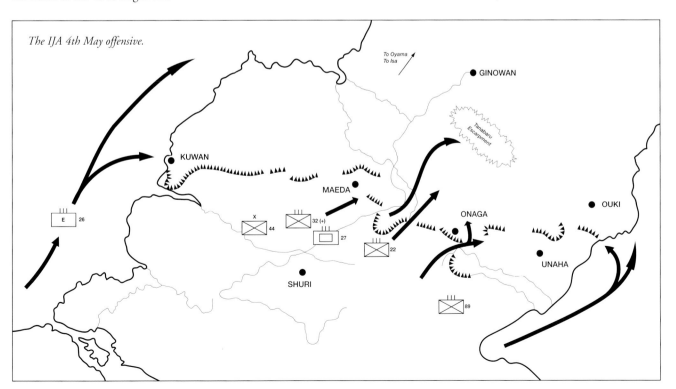

The IJA 4th May offensive.

Above: Harassing fire directed towards Japanese positions in Southern Okinawa during the early morning hours of 11th May 1945.

Above right: A USMC OY-1 Sentinel observation aircraft flies low over Naha, the capital city of Okinawa.

Meanwhile, the 44th IMB was in position northwest of Shuri ready to begin its drive toward Oyama as soon as the 32nd Regiment opened a breach in the American lines. Dismayed by the heavy casualties and by the failure of the 24th Division's attacks, Major-General Suzuki, commander of the 44th IMB, asked to be thrown into the assault. Yahara told him, however, that as the area on Maeda hill was not yet sufficiently cleared of the enemy for the 44th to move, it would only heighten the needless sacrifice and still not achieve a strategic breakthrough.

On the night of 4th–5th May, the 32nd Regiment of the 24th Division, achieved an unexpected success. Its 1st Battalion, under Captain Ito Koichi, had, on its own initiative, abandoned the hopeless frontal attacks it was ordered to make during the day and instead spent its time carefully reconnoitring the American positions. This allowed it during the night to infiltrate eastward across the Ginowan–Shuri road undetected and then to penetrate

half a mile into the American rear to the Tanabaru escarpment. By dawn on 5th May, Ito's battalion held Tanabaru in force.

Captain Ito's brilliant results based upon faulty orders were not an accident. He had come to the conclusion that, since there were so few radios in use, the 32nd Army staff based their orders on reports carried by runners which were received some time after events had taken place. The orders were based on false assumptions of where the front line was, a recurring problem because the front line was irregular, having numerous gaps, and constantly shifting. Ito thus acquired the habit of reconnoitring along his battalion's front line each night to discover where his and the Americans' positions were. This allowed him to adjust his response to orders in the most appropriate way to the actual situation. This method, although unorthodox, stood Ito's battalion in good stead on 4th May.

The IJA 27th Tank Regiment was also active in the Maeda hill sector at the left end of the 24th Division's line. This was the only occasion where the Japanese used tanks in an offensive role on Okinawa. The tank regiment had little success trying to break through at Maeda, however. It penetrated to the far side of the Maeda heights on 5th May but was unable to contact the infantry unit there that was supposed to support it in the joint attack. It therefore returned to its 4th May positions. Some Japanese observers felt the 27th Tank Regiment had achieved an advantageous position on Maeda hill during 4th May and that it and the supporting infantry elements in the area therefore ought not to have been recalled the next day. Nevertheless, when the 27th Tank Regiment did withdraw, it had only six tanks remaining, all of which were then converted to earth-covered pillboxes southwest of Shuri.

The 26th and 23rd Shipping Engineer Regiments fared even worse than the tank units. The 26th Engineers were supposed to move up the west coast on the night of 3rd–4th May and land at Oyama, well behind the American lines. There they were to link up with the 44th IMB when it swept into Oyama. The 26th Shipping Engineer Regiment mistook its position, however, and turned into the coast at Kuwan, a point lying just behind the American front line and heavily defended. At 02:00, elements of the US 1st Marine Division opened fire with machine guns on the barges of the 26th Engineers trying to reach shore over the reefs. All of the boats were destroyed, and the few IJA soldiers who reached Kuwan were easily mopped up. Soldiers of the 26th landed farther north at Isa, but these also were easily wiped-out.

The 23rd Shipping Engineer Regiment, moving along the east coast at the same time, did no better. It landed just behind the US 7th Infantry Division line near Ouki as planned but having landed on the flat coastland was easily contained and destroyed by the 7th Division.

The Japanese staff, however, had no knowledge of these disasters, as the shipping units were in too much disarray to report. During the morning of 4th May the staff still assumed the counter-landing forces were enjoying success, and on 5th May these units were recalled, though by that time, unknown to the Japanese staff, they had ceased to exist. They 'disregarded the order and fought to the last man', as an IJA staff officer later put it, though, in fact, they had 'fought to the last man' the day before.

By 5th May the forward movement of the 24th Division's offensive had completely stopped. The weakened 62nd Division on the western half of the isthmus had not been able to move at all. The 44th IMB, though poised for action, was not even sent on its planned arc northwest to Oyama. The only bright spot was that, at dawn, the 1st Battalion of the 32nd Regiment, 24th Division, under Captain Ito, held the Tanabaru escarpment.

When the 1st Battalion reached the Tanabaru heights, it sent a visual light signal to 32nd Army, since its radio cryptographers had been lost. But Colonel Yahara doubted on the basis of this one signal that they were really there. Since Yahara controlled operations, this guaranteed that Ito's battalion would remain unsupported and isolated; Yahara always erred on the side of caution.

Somehow Ito survived. At dawn on 5th May, the American forces counter-attacked Ito and a fierce battle ensued that lasted

two days. Ito's battalion dug in on the heights, reoccupied the caves in the area, and vigorously defended them when the US 17th Infantry Regiment counter-attacked. The Japanese used machine guns, mortars, grenades, and a 75mm pack howitzer they had brought with them, as well as captured American weapons. They cut telephone wires between the 17th Infantry Regiment and its battalions and cut off all access of that regiment to its own rear through the town of Tanabaru. On the night of the 6th, Ito's men made their way back to Japanese lines in accord with an order issued to them at noon on 6th May. The 17th Infantry Regiment calculated that Ito's 1st Battalion, 32nd Regiment, had lost 462 men.

Overall, the news on 5th May was so discouraging that, at 18:00, Ushijima, the 32nd Army commander, took it on himself to suspend the entire offensive and recalled all units to their pre-4th May positions. He thus spared Cho and other staff officers from having to make this humiliating decision. Ushijima summoned Yahara and told him of the planned retreat. That night, the order was sent by coded radio signals to all units. Ushijima told Yahara that Yahara had been right after all, that the attack had failed, and that he would give Yahara more latitude in the future. He said that he had promised Field Marshal Hajime Sugiyama, War Minister in the Kuniaki Koiso cabinet, and IJA Chief of Staff Umezu that he would not execute a premature honourable death attack and that, although the army had suffered heavy casualties, he would fight on with the remaining forces. Cho also rose to this occasion and helped soothe the anger and frustration of Jin and the others over halting the attack on which so much had been gambled. The young staff officers gave in temporarily to tears of despair.

The casualties suffered in the 4th May offensive were quite large, even though there were no operational gains. In two days, the 32nd Army had lost 7,000 men of its original 76,000-man force. The 62nd Division had only 25 per cent of its strength remaining, the 24th Division 60 per cent, and the 44th IMB 80 per cent. Moreover, the capability of the 5th Artillery Command was sharply reduced. Many of its pieces were lost because they were moved out of their caves toward the front lines to give better support for the offensive. Besides that, a large volume of shells had been expended so that the daily ration of shells per gun was reduced from 50 to 15 per day. Overall, artillery firepower was thus reduced to about 50 per cent of its original strength.

All in all, while the 4th–5th May offensive was a catastrophe, it was a brilliant catastrophe in the sense that it was a bold and imaginative stroke. It was useful for morale before it happened because it gave hope to staff members who were aware of the

Above: US Marines pick their way through the debris of the ancient castle of Shuri.

Above right: American tank crews on Naha airstrip planning the final details of an advance on the sea wall.

plans for it. It also may have had some value in keeping American commanders off balance, forcing them to keep more units back to guard the rear areas, though there is little evidence of this. A bold surprise is often advantageous in a campaign, even against long odds. That proved not to be the case for the 4th May offensive, however. The Japanese lost scarce troops and material and, from then on, would have to rely more and more on service and support troops who had been converted to fight in the front line. The spirit of hope was also a casualty. A pall of gloom settled back on the 32nd Army staff after the 4th May offensive, and it never lifted.

The 29th May Withdrawal

After the suspension of the 4th May offensive, American forces again took the initiative and made deep incursions into the Japanese lines along both the east and west coasts. By 22nd May, the 32nd Army staff was again debating what should be done. The answer that ultimately emerged was that all of 32nd Army

would withdraw to the Kiyan Peninsula in the south, form a new line, and fight on. The withdrawal would demonstrate two characteristic features of 32nd Army's performance: first, its being torn still between romantic self-sacrifice and rational economy of force, and second, its aptitude for deft and effective manoeuvre in difficult circumstances.

After the failure of the 4th May offensive, 32nd Army's only plan was to hold its position. Since that approach was failing, Cho and others decided an appeal should be made to IGHQ for a massive air attack on the American fleet that would disrupt the US Tenth Army's supply and cause its advance to falter. Major Jin was ordered on 10th May to carry this plea to Tokyo. Jin was also to report on the state of affairs on Okinawa and the lessons learned from the fighting. Yahara, although he did not interfere, opposed this plan on the grounds that with six divisions ashore, the American campaign would not be much affected by such additional air support as IGHQ could muster. The ten waves of kamikaze attacks already launched on US shipping around Okinawa had had only a limited effect on the ground fighting. Moreover, Yahara felt it would appear self-serving to ask that planes husbanded for the final defence of the homeland be used up instead on the Okinawa campaign. Yahara nonetheless attended Jin's farewell at Shuri and gave him a notebook to deliver to his father-in-law, a retired IJA lieutenant-general. Jin

was supposed to return to Tokyo by seaplane, but when the plane was unable to put down because of rough water, he set out by night in an ordinary fishing boat. The main result of Jin's voyage to Tokyo was that he himself, a leading advocate of sacrificial attack, survived the Okinawa campaign. News of his safe arrival in Tokyo caused some ambivalent feelings among his colleagues who remained in harm's way.

Soon after Jin's departure, another sign appeared indicating that 32nd Army's days were numbered. Several dozen young women were present in the Shuri cave headquarters, as they might be in any secure IJA office facility, working at routine clerical tasks. The staff members felt that, although it was their duty to die with the army, it was not the duty of these young women to do so. The women were therefore ordered to make their way out of the Shuri underground position and rejoin the civilians of the Okinawa population. The young women protested that they were prepared to die when they came to the headquarters and that they were being sent away just because they were women. Nonetheless, they were made to feel they had to obey the commander's order and leave. As they scrambled out of the cave with their rucksacks in tow, the soldiers shouted after them things like 'you may get yourself killed, but don't let anything happen to that fabulous face'. This helped relieve the tension for a while. Ushijima and Cho, sensing the end, gave the young women as personal gifts their few treasured items of fine ceramic ware.

Meanwhile, the US Tenth Army resumed its offensive on 11th May. Through sustained pressure and hard fighting for particular objectives such as Conical Hill on the east coast and Sugar Loaf on the west coast, the Americans pushed the whole Japanese line back half a mile by 21st May. They achieved especially deep lodgements on the two extreme flanks, which was their intention. Especially on the eastern flank, elements of the US 96th Infantry Division had probed as far as Sugar Loaf Hill and were close to turning the Japanese flank at Yonabaru.

The 32nd Army faced the same situation it had in mid-April. Its line was crumbling at both ends and about to collapse. This time, however, there were no reserves available to bring forward, once more placing the 32nd Army staff in a dilemma. Yahara, who had responsibility for the army's operations, felt withdrawal to the Kiyan Peninsula would be best. By this time, however, his relations with Cho had become so adversarial that he dared not even mention this solution. Instead he arranged for a junior staff member, Major Nagano Hideo, to submit to Cho a short position paper that spelled out pros and cons but tended to favour the Kiyan withdrawal. Cho characteristically preferred an unyielding defence of the Shuri area where the 32nd Army already was.

To resolve the question, Cho convened a meeting of all major unit chiefs of staff on 22nd May. The meeting considered three proposals. The first was to encircle Shuri and prepare a concentrated defence. Such a position, however, would be too small to hold the 50,000 surviving troops and the many long-range guns that were still intact. Moreover, such a restricted area would be extremely vulnerable to artillery fire.

The second option considered was to withdraw from the Shuri line to the Chinen Peninsula. The Chinen was favourable as defensive terrain. It offered obstacles to easy tank movement and was encircled by sea and cliffs that would make amphibious envelopment more difficult. But the Chinen did not have good road access, which would hamper Japanese transport. Besides that, the Americans, who were already breaking through on the east, threatened the withdrawal routes to the eastward-lying Chinen Peninsula. The main difficulty with the Chinen, however, was that its defences had been developed earlier by the 44th IMB. It therefore did not have caves enough or stored stockpiles enough to accommodate the entire 32nd Army.

The third possibility was to withdraw and form a line across the Kiyan Peninsula. The Kiyan had two defensible peaks, Yaeju-Dake and Yuza-Dake. Much of the coastal front was protected by 100–130 feet high precipices to frustrate amphibious landings in the rear. Having been developed by the larger 24th Division, the Kiyan had caves and stockpiles enough to provide for the entire 32nd Army. The major disadvantage was that much of the terrain was open and flat, thus allowing tanks to move freely. This terrain defect was the more serious since by this time 32nd Army's anti-tank guns and mines, and for that matter its best anti-tank soldiers, had already been lost.

Each chief of staff at the 22nd May meeting was asked which alternative his unit favoured. Colonel Ueno, chief of staff of the 62nd Division, spoke first, in urgent tones. He said that the 62nd Division had nearly exhausted its resources, above ground and below, and lacked the energy and means for a withdrawal. Moreover, the division had several thousand wounded that it

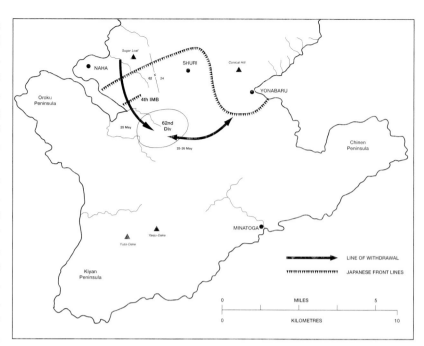

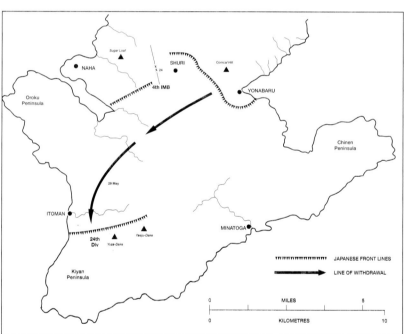

could not consider leaving behind. Therefore, the men in the 62nd Division wished to be allowed honourable death on the Shuri line. Most of their friends had already died there. The other 32nd Army staff officers, hearing Colonel Ueno's plea, were deeply moved.

The chief of staff of the 24th Division, Colonel Kitani, then spoke, describing the advantages of moving the army to the Kiyan Peninsula. He pointed out that the 24th Division's 24th Transport

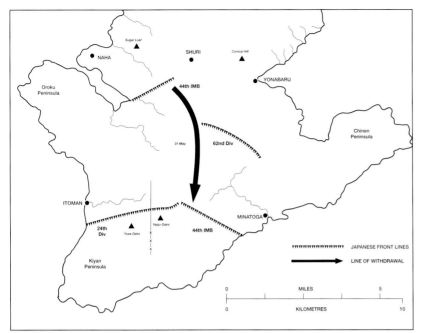

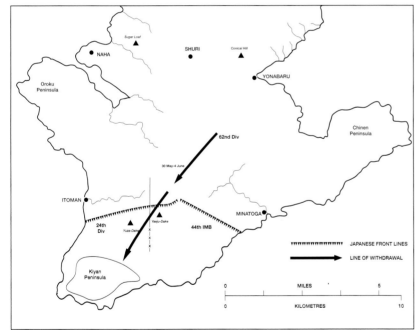

Above left: *Preliminary withdrawal of the 62nd Division, 25th May.*

Below left: *Withdrawal of the 24th Division, 29th May.*

Top: *Withdrawal of the 44th Independent Mixed Brigade, 31st May.*

Above: *Final withdrawal of the 62nd Division, 4th June.*

Regiment still had 80 trucks intact that could be used to move the army. A staff officer of the 44th IMB then gave his opinion in favour of moving the army to the Chinen Peninsula. In fact, each unit's chief of staff wished the new line placed in the area where each unit had developed its own respective fortifications before the battle began. Each unit apparently wished to fight on familiar ground and in familiar defences.

After the meeting was dismissed Yahara took his recommendation to Cho. It had not been altered by the meeting. He still believed that 32nd Army should withdraw to a new line across the Kiyan Peninsula. He challenged the point of view of Colonel Ueno and the 62nd Division that they should fight on around Shuri. He said that seeking honourable death at Shuri because comrades had died there was pure sentimentality. The Shuri position, once surrounded, would be indefensible and a military disaster would follow. Okinawa forces would fail to delay the coming struggle for the homeland. To die for such a reason and with no good results was barbaric. The army's policy had to be realistic, and that meant moving to the Kiyan Peninsula.

Yahara was evidently braced for another struggle with Cho over whether spiritual or operational priorities should prevail. This turned out to be unnecessary; the likeable and unpredictable Cho straightforwardly agreed with the recommendation and wisely refrained from commenting on the argument. Retreat to Kiyan thus became 32nd Army's policy on the next day, 23rd May, when endorsed by General Ushijima. Movement of the wounded and munitions was to begin at once.

The 32nd Army staff was eager to conduct the retreat from Shuri in such a way that the Americans did not break through the Shuri line and destroy the Japanese forces in detail while they were moving. In fact the Japanese would be so successful at this that the Americans had no idea a retreat was taking place until the day before it was completed. The 32nd Army staff was especially concerned that the Americans' deep inroads along the east coast near Yonabaru might produce an American breakthrough at the east end of the line. The US 77th Infantry Division in that case could sweep westward and cut off the Japanese retreat, thus encircling large portions of the Japanese force, which would be caught in the open.

To prevent this, the remaining men of the 62nd Division were to withdraw behind the Shuri lines on 25th May and attack the Yonabaru salient, thus containing the US 77th Infantry Division and pushing it back away from the retreat routes (see map 9). This would allow the retreat of the main units on 29th May. In the event 62nd Division withdrew south of Shuri on the night of 24th–25th May and attacked American positions at Yonabaru on the night of 25th–26th May. This did not push back the Americans, but it did slow the US 77th Infantry Division's forward progress and prevented its achieving an untimely breakthrough. The impression this made on the American commanders, who were unaware of the imminent retreat, was that the Japanese were fighting fiercely to maintain existing lines.

After the east flank was somewhat stabilised, the 24th Division pulled back from the northeast part of the line to the southwest on 29th May (see map 10). The 44th IMB pulled away from the northwest part of the line to the southeast on 31st May (see map 11). The 62nd Division completed its withdrawal from its intermediate lines south of Shuri to a reserve area south of the new Kiyan lines on 4th June (see map 12). The 24th Division was also required to leave behind a screening force, which fell back to successively southward positions according to a timetable, reaching the Kiyan position also on 4th June.

The withdrawal of 29th May – 4th June was completed in an orderly way, and the American forces did not inflict heavy losses in their pursuit. These advantages were achieved by the retreat's being carefully planned and because the spring rainy season began in the last week of May, a little later and harder than usual. This hampered American tanks and reconnaissance aircraft. The rains also hampered the Japanese transport during the retreat, however, and turned the shafts of IJA caves into 'small rivers'. All of the Japanese movements were carried out under cover of darkness, and the 24th Transport Regiment of the 24th Division performed yeoman service with its 80 trucks.

The Japanese withdrawal to fresh lines in the south succeeded in part because the Americans did not make an early concerted effort to break through the screening forces at Shuri. On 26th May American aerial observers noted men, artillery, and armour moving south, but they also reported a large column moving north. This latter force was probably the IJA rear-area garrison units that were moved from the Chinen Peninsula to aid in the 25th–26th May attacks on Yonabaru. Since the American analysts were not aware of an overall pattern of southerly movement, they

concluded that the Japanese were using the bad weather to cover an overdue rotation of reserve and front-line troops.

Visibility on 29th May was zero, and air observation was impossible. Nevertheless, by 30th May, because of recently abandoned IJA positions found west of Shuri and other accumulating pieces of evidence, Tenth Army intelligence finally reached a consensus that the Shuri lines were being abandoned. But the Americans did not know where the new lines were and assumed they were about two miles behind the old ones, just enough to straighten out the salients the Americans had built up on the east and west.

American forces moved into Shuri on 31st May, completing the reduction of the formidable Shuri line. They realised by this time that they were dealing only with a rearguard. The American force prepared to pursue the Japanese southward on 1st June, but by this time, the 44th IMB, the last IJA unit in the vicinity, had already completed its withdrawal. Moreover, given the well

Above: US Marines move in on the ruins of a Japanese barracks on the outskirts of Shuri.

Nonetheless, the IJA losses in the execution of this operation were staggering. When the 32nd Army staff took stock on 4th June of forces on hand, there were only 30,000 men left of the 50,000 men who had been present two weeks before. The 32nd Army had lost 40 per cent of its personnel in the one-week retreat, some through the 62nd Division's aggressive attacks against the Americans at Yonabaru, some by the interdiction and harassing artillery fire directed at the roads the Japanese were using, some in the countless and hopeless rearguard actions. Although historians have never made much of this, one must wonder if the smoothly executed retreat was really well advised or that it allowed the Japanese to resist for a longer period. Yahara, who condemned the heavy losses, 7,000 men, of the 4th May offensive he opposed, had no self-criticism for the far heavier losses of the 29th May retreat that he sponsored.

IJA staff officers noted that the 30,000 men who did survive now included few trained combat troops. Only 20 per cent of the combat troops present on 1st April were still able to fight. Most of the personnel surviving after 4th June were service, support and construction troops. Moreover, the retreat resulted in heavy losses of infantry weapons other than personal firearms. Only 20 per cent of the machine guns and 10 per cent of the heavier weapons survived. Hand grenades and mines were now almost exhausted. Only the large field guns that were kept in the rear with the 5th Artillery Command were relatively unscathed. Half of these were still intact, including 16 x 150mm howitzers.

Officers of the upper echelons also survived. Though company officers serving in the front line companies were almost wiped out, battalion commanders and their staffs were nearly untouched. All but 14 battalion level staff members were still at their posts on 4th June. This allowed for maximum organisational cohesion in spite of the heavy losses on the line. Even so, these men were becoming increasingly exposed by the savage fighting, a staff without an army.

The 32nd Army on the Kiyan Peninsula was, in men and weapons, a very weakened force, an army aware that its days of organised resistance were numbered. The army's final drama was played out in microcosm by the Okinawa Naval Base Force on Oroku Peninsula between 26th May and 13th June. The Naval Base Force, under Rear-Admiral Ota Minoru, was located from the beginning of the campaign on Oroku Peninsula where it defended the naval port and air station. This force had developed elaborate seaward coastal defences in cave emplacements and also land defence fortifications as other units had on Okinawa.

protected nature of the Japanese defences, it was impossible for the Americans to move forward safely if even a few Japanese remained in the pillbox caves. Those last few had to be eliminated, and that inevitably took days. The problem remained even after the Shuri line fell, because the 62nd Division and the 24th Division's rearguard both manned intermediate positions between Shuri and the Kiyan area. Even though the IJA screening forces were few, safe and rapid forward pursuit by the Americans was impossible. In the upshot, Tenth Army units were not ready to engage the new Kiyan lines until 6th June.

The Japanese thus succeeded in moving all their units intact to the south, and the Americans were unable to effect the rapid pursuit strategists dream of and destroy the 32nd Army.

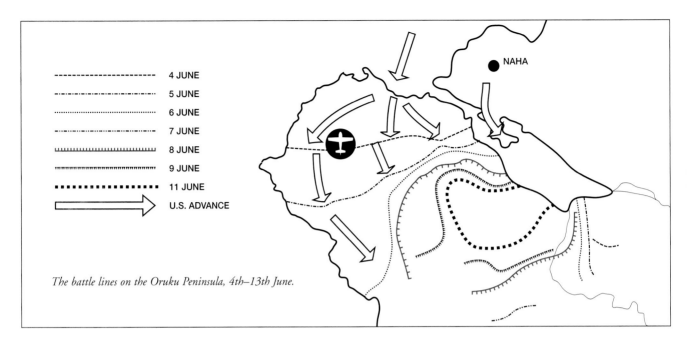

The battle lines on the Oruku Peninsula, 4th–13th June.

There were 8,825 IJN officers and sailors in the Naval Base Force as well as 1,100 Okinawan Home Guards, a total of 9,925 men. Of this total, however, only a few hundred had been initially trained and equipped for ground fighting. All the rest were signals, torpedo maintenance, naval stores, and similar personnel. In short, the Oroku naval detachment, although it faced a seasoned ground combat force, was not one itself.

On 26th May, as orders for the retreat to the Kiyan were being disseminated, the Naval Base Force received a radio message stating that it should destroy its heavy weapons and withdraw to the Kiyan Peninsula on 2nd June. Ota misinterpreted the order, however, and moved his force to the Kiyan on 28th May. Almost immediately after reaching the new positions in the Kiyan, however, the naval force returned to its former base on Oroku without permission. Apparently, the Naval Base Force staff did not like the new positions and wished during their last stand to occupy the more familiar positions they had prepared and in that part of the island that had traditionally belonged to the Navy. The 32nd Army staff, on hearing these sentiments expressed by Ota, was pleased to authorise the naval forces' return to the Oroku base after the fact, despite having just ordered them to leave it. The 32nd Army accounts of this episode vary, but one may assume 32nd Army was trying to alleviate its very serious faux pas of having ordered the Naval Base Force to die in Army lines rather than defending its own base.

The US 6th Marine Division landed on Oroku's north coast on the morning of 4th June, and a pitched battle ensued that lasted ten days. The Okinawa Naval Base Force in the few days since its return to Oroku had resumed the defensive positions it had spent months preparing. The attacking US Marines faced caves and well-sited machine-gun nests, just as they had on the Shuri line.

Although few of these IJN troops were trained for ground warfare, they were extremely resourceful in converting air and anti-ship equipment to ground use. The Japanese used 200mm naval guns against tanks and fired 200mm anti-ship rockets into the Marines' lines. The Marines called the rockets 'locomotives from hell' because of the terrible noise they made, though, like the 320mm mortars, they caused few casualties due to the lack of fragmentation on exploding. The Naval Base Force also used mines and mortars abundantly against the advancing Marines. Perhaps most effective, however, was its deployment of 252 machine guns, many of them taken from damaged aircraft. Even though this was not a force trained for ground combat, its resourcefulness and ample equipment allowed it to inflict casualties on the Americans at a rate comparable to that on the Shuri line.

Even so, the US 6th Marine Division pushed the Japanese Naval Base Force back down the peninsula and encircled it at the northeast end of the peninsula's base by 11th June (see map 13). Ota sent his farewell telegram to 32nd Army on 11th June, and his headquarters sent its last signal to 32nd Army at 16:00 on 12th June. The IJN line broke on 12th June, and by 13th June organised resistance by the IJN had ceased. Some 159 members of the Japanese Naval Base Force surrendered, the first time this occurred on Okinawa. Rear-Admiral Ota Minoru and five of his aides committed suicide in the Oroku headquarters cave at 01:00 on 13th June.

CHAPTER 5 The Last Days, June 1945

The IJA's new Kiyan peninsula line was largely in place by 3rd June. The American forces had formed a line opposite it by 6th June and began their probing attacks on the east flank. The American forces did not reach the west part of the line until 9th June, being reluctant to move forward until the Oroku pocket was isolated, and did not attack in the west until 12th June, when the Oroku fighting had finished. The Americans formed a continuous line, though the west end of the line did not approach the Japanese western positions until several days after contact had been made in the east. The advance was deliberate and cautious, so that they reached the Japanese line with the full benefit of their organisation and firepower.

The Japanese position was about five miles across and four miles deep. It was anchored along a line running from Kunishi Ridge in the west through Yuza-Dake and Yaeju-Dake peaks, to Hanagusuku village and Hill 95 on the east (see map 14). Manning this line from Kunishi to Yaeju-Dake were the 24th Division's 32nd and 89th Regiments. The 24th Division set its headquarters at Medeera and held its 22nd Regiment in reserve at nearby Makabe. Manning the line on the east, from Yaeju-Dake to the sea, were the 44th IMB's newly formed 6th Specially Established Regiment and the 15th Independent Mixed Regiment (IMR). The 44th IMB headquarters was placed above the coastal cliffs at Mabuni. Remnants of the 62nd Division were held as a reserve at the southernmost tip of the peninsula. The 32nd Army's new headquarters was at Mabuni near that of the 44th IMB.

Above: Red Beach, Iheya Shima, 3rd June.

The arithmetic of units was now becoming crucial for the 32nd Army staff, because they were simply running out of men. The US 7th Infantry Division pushed hard at the two ends of the 44th IMB position, at the Yaeju-Dake end and at the ridge running northeast from Hill 95. From 9th to 11th June, the Americans made a concerted attack against the centre around Azato village and against Hill 95 on the east, resulting in their capture of Hill 95 on 11th June.

On the night of 11th–12th June, the 3rd Battalion of the US 17th Infantry Regiment accomplished a night infiltration that ejected the IJA 6th Specially Established Regiment from the eastern foot of Yaeju-Dake. The 6th Specially Established Regiment was untried and had few combat soldiers in it. It had occupied the eastern foot of Yaeju-Dake rather than the summit, as ordered, because it could obtain no water on the summit.

By 12th June American forces had penetrated both flanks of the 44th IMB portion of the Kiyan line, thus threatening also the east flank of the 24th Division's section of the line. Under these circumstances, the 32nd Army staff hastened to send in its last reserves to stem the American advance. On 11th June, soon after the American attacks began in earnest on 9th June, the 32nd Army staff had already rushed some reinforcements to the critical Yaeju-Dake area. These were assorted small units, equal to about six companies, that 32nd Army headquarters had on hand. They were drawn from the 5th Artillery units, a signal

Main photograph: *2nd Marine Division's 8th Marines returned to Okinawa on 30th May. The 2nd and 3rd Battalions landed on Iheya Shima on 3rd June. Here LVTs approach Red Beach during the landings.*

Inset: *US Marines of 2nd Division on Iheya.*

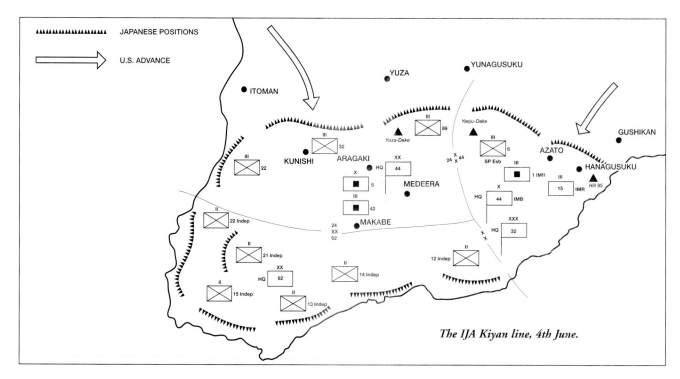

The IJA Kiyan line, 4th June.

unit, and a field fortification unit. Unfortunately, because these troops were 'poorly equipped as well as inadequately trained', they suffered heavy casualties on contact, and their efforts were 'as ineffective as throwing water on parched soil'.

After the fall of Yaeju-Dake to the Americans on 12th June, the commander of the 24th Division made urgent pleas to 32nd Army to recapture it and so secure 24th Division's exposed right flank. Therefore, on 13th June, the 32nd Army ordered the 15th Independent Infantry Battalion to drive the Americans out of

the Yaeju-Dake area and the 13th Independent Infantry Battalion to attack the Americans on the extreme right, in the vicinity of Hill 95. Both of these battalions belonged to the 62nd Division, the 32nd Army's last reserve. These attacks, however, had almost no success. The 13th Independent Infantry Battalion promptly moved up to the line on the extreme right but lost more than half of its fighting strength on the first day. This was in part because the Americans had already taken Hill 95, leaving little terrain cover to the advancing 13th.

Above: 8th Marines' 1st Battalion landed on Aguni Shima on 9th June. This photograph shows their Amtracs after the landing.

Below left: Amtracs approach the beach on Aguni.

The 15th Independent Infantry Battalion was not able even to reach the front quickly. The 24th Division commander protested the delay, and Yahara gave a direct order from the 32nd Army to the 15th Independent Infantry Battalion commander to attack immediately. This kind of order, outside the chain of command, was almost unheard of. Even so, the 15th Battalion was unable to advance. It encountered American tanks as it tried to move out of its reserve area toward Yaeju-Dake and did not have a single anti-tank gun. The commander,

Major Iizuka, was himself wounded, and he commanded his battalion from a stretcher. The upshot was that the Americans secured their hold on Yaeju-Dake beyond retrieval.

By 15th June, with both flanks already staved in, the 44th IMB's line was broken into fragments. Therefore, the 32nd Army ordered the remainder of the 62nd Division reserve force into the 44th IMB's zone. The 62nd Division's commander, Lieutenant-General Nakajima Gen, was given command of the 44th IMB as well as his own division. By 16th June the remainder of the 62nd Division had made very slow progress toward the east, however, because of 'unfamiliar terrain, darkness, and furious enemy shelling'. Meanwhile, the extreme right flank unit of the 44th IMB, the 15th Independent Mixed Regiment, had lost contact with other units, and its headquarters was under attack by American tanks.

By 17th June, the 44th IMB had fallen back to a new line running southeast from Yuza-Dake to the sea. This was held more thinly than the Yaeju-Dake–Hanagusuku line, but was at least continuous. The 62nd Division intended to form a line

behind this point, then advance to it. But the 62nd Division had still made so little progress that it was ordered directly by 32nd Army to advance its line as far as Mabuni, that is, to within half a mile of where the 44th's line was. This movement was only completed on 18th June. The 62nd Division's 64th Infantry Brigade held the sector running from Yuza-Dake southeast to a point east of Medeera, and 63nd Infantry Brigade held the sector running from a point east of Medeera to a point east of Mabuni and the sea.

While the 44th IMB's front was being pushed back to Yuza-Dake–Mabuni between 6th and 18th June, the 24th Division's front was also hard pressed. Because the Naval Base Force fighting on Oroku threatened the Americans' west flank, they were slower to probe forward on the west, the 24th Division's sector. By 11th June, however, the Americans had passed through all the rearguard resistance and had also subdued Oroku. They attacked the whole length of the 24th Division line, Kunishi–Yuza-Dake, on 12th June, after the east flank fighting had already been under way for six days.

From 12th to 17th June, the 24th Division's 32nd and 89th Infantry Regiments sturdily held their ground against continuous attacks by the US 1st Marine Division and part of the US 96th Infantry Division. Here the Japanese resistance still showed the quality it had had on the Shuri line. Relying on well prepared caves and the high ground of Kunishi Ridge and Yuza-Dake, and having still a fair amount of trained manpower, the 24th Division did not budge for five days, despite the usual bludgeoning by infantry–tank groups and fierce land, sea, and air saturation bombardment.

The searing pattern of assault and counter-attack typical of the Shuri fighting still appeared here. The US Marines assaulted Yuza village for many days only to be driven out on as many nights. Before dawn on 12th June, two companies of the US 7th Marine Regiment reached the crest of Kunishi Ridge itself, but at daylight, they were fiercely counter-attacked and their communications cut off by the mortaring and shelling of the north face of the ridge they had just come up. Casualties in these isolated American companies were heavy, but they were nevertheless built up into a survivable fighting force in the next five days by the precarious expedient of the supplies being brought up by tanks. Tanks brought reinforcements, plasma, and ammunition when they came up and carried out the wounded when they left. Any other movement across the deadly north slope area was impossible, because IJA 24th Division elements still held parts of the ridge and points east of the ridge so that they could cover its whole face with fire. Things were no better for the Americans on the crest of the ridge. They could not stand up without being shot so that even the wounded had to be dragged on ponchos to the escape hatches under the tanks. The tanks themselves, which came up each day to fight for the enlargement of the perimeter, were subject to 47mm anti-tank fire on the road, both coming and going. Some 21 American tanks were destroyed in the five days of fighting for Kunishi Ridge.

The Japanese line east of Yaeju-Dake fell back a mile between 12th and 18th June, while the line west of Yaeju-Dake held rock steady. The reason for this discrepancy was that the east end of the line was engaged six days before the west end, but also lay in part in the west end's having a greater number of trained men and weapons than the east had. Thanks largely to a copious addition of replacements from service support troops to the line divisions, the 24th Division on the west had 12,000 men, equal

Above left: Troops advance into Aguni.

Left: 8th Marines at Aguni Shima, 20 miles west of Okinawa on 9th June. The island is wreathed in smoke from the pre-invasion bombardment.

Above: *Near miss for a US M4 during the fighting for Naha where organized enemy resistance ended on 20th June.*

to 85 per cent of its original strength. The east flank's 44th IMB had 3,000 troops, equal to 67 per cent of its original numbers, while the 62nd Division had 7,000, equal to about 60 per cent of its initial muster.

By 18th June, a majority of the units fighting east of Yaeju-Dake were already reorganised into rear-area units with few light weapons and almost no heavy ones. The 6th Specially Established Regiment, fighting on the 44th's left, for example, was a newly reconstituted regiment, not a trained combat regiment, and was made up entirely of rear-area personnel. The same was true of the remnant of the 62nd Division that was sent to help the 44th. The 60 per cent of the 62nd's original strength level still on the line was not the 62nd's original line combat component but made up from untrained replacements. As these forces went in on the Japanese right, they were 'indignantly

assaulting enemy tanks with clenched teeth and naked fists', as one IJA staff officer put it. The problem east of Yaeju-Dake was not a problem of morale but simply a matter of the units there having reached the end of their resources, in numbers, weapons, and combat-trained leaders. This exhaustion of resources came a few days earlier on the IJA right than on the left because the Americans attacked sooner on the right and because the IJA units on the right were more battle-worn.

Some small efforts were made to solve the Japanese armaments problem between 12th and 17th June. Several plane loads of hand grenades and grenade launchers were parachuted in by the 6th Air Army. The garrison on Tokuno Island, which had seen no fighting, sent five small boats of ammunition to the beleaguered 32nd Army, but though they successfully negotiated the long sea voyage, they were sunk within sight of 32nd Army's Kiyan position.

By 18th June, the 24th Division's position on the Japanese left was also giving way. On 15th June, American units had penetrated an area between Yaeju-Dake and Yuza-Dake in the

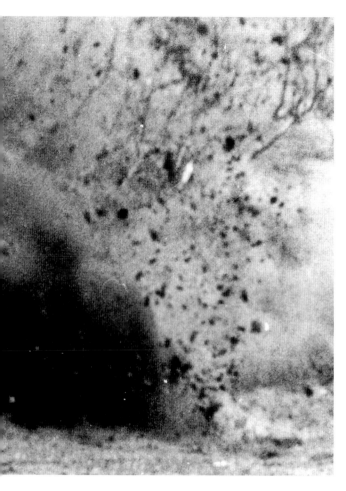

but its front remained intact. Meanwhile, the regimental headquarters was attacked from the rear by American infantry–tank groups. For four days, these attacks were repulsed. By the evening of 22nd June, however, the Regiment's battalions and its headquarters were separately enveloped and communications between them disrupted. Within a few days, the 32nd Regiment, in turn, had ceased to exist as a fighting force. By 22nd June, nothing remained of the 24th Division except the division headquarters troops around Medeera and such stragglers from the line regiments as had reached there.

All of 24th Division, like the rest of the 32nd Army on the Kiyan Peninsula, suffered from lack of trained soldiers and arms. Combat ranks were badly thinned, so each regiment was reconstituted in the lull just after the arrival at the new Kiyan line. Medical, veterinary, supply, and other personnel were brought in to make good the losses. As a result, the line units consisted of men with a variety of specialties, none of which was combat.

The Japanese shortage of weapons was telling. Men impressed from the rear had no weapons and were given none. Each reconstituted 24th Division battalion had to make do with 80 rifles, five light machine guns, and five grenade launchers. Even the machine-gun companies had only three to five machine guns each, and regimental gun companies had only two guns in each. Moreover, not all of this scarce equipment was in good condition. Limited troop numbers, experience, and equipment all help to explain the abrupt dissolution of the 24th Division's line regiments between 17th and 22nd June.

By 19th June, it was apparent to the 32nd Army staff and its commander, General Ushijima, that neither the west nor the east sectors of the army's line would hold. The staff therefore began doing some formal, but nevertheless important, things to prepare for the end of the army. On 10th June, a unit citation bearing Ushijima's signature had already been awarded to the 24th Division for its achievements on the Shuri line and in the 4th May offensive. Now, on 19th June, Ushijima's last order to the army congratulated all units on their performance. But, he noted, the army's weapons were nearly expended, and communications between units had been severed. Therefore, wherever communications were broken, the senior officer of any unit was authorised to command it without waiting on orders from a superior. All members of the army were to 'fight to the last'. Ushijima's last order made no mention of surrender.

The 19th June order tidied up matters with respect to the subordinate units, but formalities toward superiors also had to be observed. On the evening of 18th June, Ushijima sent his farewell message to the Vice-Chief of Staff of the IJA, Kawanabe Torashiro, and to the commander of the 10th Area Army on

middle of the 89th Regiment's front. This led, on 19th June, to the death in the fighting near Aragaki of almost all officers and men of the 89th.

On 13th June the 22nd Regiment was brought up from its reserve position in the rear, shortly after American attacks began in earnest on the 12th. On 17th June the American strength in the far left of 24th Division's sector doubled when the 6th Marine Division, having finished fighting at Oroku, took over the western half of the 1st Marine Division's line. The entire 22nd Regiment line collapsed under the weight of the reinforced Marine assault. The whole unit was overrun and wiped out. The regimental headquarters was surrounded, and almost all of its staff, including the commander, died in action.

The 32nd Regiment in the centre still held out, even though its left flank was completely unhinged where the 22nd Regiment had been until 17th June. The US Marines had already moved south through Maezato village by dusk of the 17th and were 1,000 yards in the left rear of the 32nd Regiment's line. By 18th June, the 32nd Regiment was fully enveloped on its left and rear,

Taiwan, Ando Rikichi. Ushijima ended his message with a poem: 'May the island's green grass, which has withered waiting for autumn, be born again in the spring in our honoured country'. This was reciprocated on 21st June when Army Minister Anami Korechika and Chief of the Army General Staff Umezu Yoshijiro sent their farewell messages back to the commander of 32nd Army. Their coded radio transmissions also revealed that Lieutenant General Simon B. Buckner Jr., the US Tenth Army commander, had been killed on 18th June. All of the 32nd Army headquarters cheered at this news, beside themselves with joy. Only Ushijima grieved over the enemy commander's death and was much perplexed to find that his entire young staff was rejoicing. Also on 20th June, the 32nd Army received a dispatch from the 10th Area Army that contained a citation for all 32nd Army.

The Death of General Buckner

On 18th June Lieutenant General Simon Bolivar Buckner, Jr., died from shrapnel wounds sustained while observing the fighting from a forward observation post in the 1st Marine Division area. Major General Roy Geiger was appointed Commander, Tenth Army as a replacement.

Right: High ranking officers and men from all branches of the service pay their last respects to General Buckner.

Inset: Two days before he was killed in action, General Buckner recorded congratulatory messages to his officers and men for their part in the Okinawa campaign.

Below: 20th April 1945, Army and Naval officers await arrival of Admiral Chester W. Nimitz at Yontan airfield.

As Ushijima and Cho attended to these formal details, the two flanks of the US forces continued to close southward like giant tongs around Medeera pocket as a pivot. By 19th June, the US Army XXIV Corps and US Marine III Amphibious Corps had pushed the 44th IMB back to a line running from Medeera to Mabuni. On the west, the 24th Division's line regiments had all been crushed or bypassed, so that the III Amphibious Corps was actually approaching Mabuni from the west. The American pincers were within two miles of closing, leaving only a narrow sliver of Okinawa in Japanese hands (see map 15). Outside this sliver, only a residual rear-area garrison force remained at the southernmost tip of the Kiyan Peninsula, which formed its perimeter north of Hill 72 and Uezato village. This small garrison group was isolated from major headquarters and would be overrun without great difficulty by the US 6th Marine Division on 21st June.

In fact, by 19th June the IJA sustained organised resistance only at two separate strongpoints. One of these was around Mabuni, where the 32nd Army headquarters had been from early June and where the 62nd Division headquarters and the remnant of the 44th IMB headquarters had now been driven. The other strongpoint was around Medeera where the 24th

Division headquarters and troops attached to it still held a perimeter. By this time, all personnel, medical, technical, and other, were being used as front-line combat troops.

On 20th June, American forces closed the tongs, and only the Mabuni and Medeera strongpoints remained. The 32nd Army staff officers at Mabuni could hear fierce tank and small-arms battles in the intervals between bombardments. The struggle could be heard in every direction, less than a mile distant. The last contact between the 32nd Army at Mabuni and the 24th Division at Medeera came by runner on 20th June.

At 12:00 on 21st June, the small-arms firing in Mabuni village, 400 yards north of the headquarters cave, suddenly died away, which meant that the headquarters guard unit, sent forward to hold the village, had been wiped out. Within two hours, headquarters guards on Hill 89 overlooking one of the entrances of the headquarters cave were attacked by elements of the US 7th Infantry Division and overrun. The Americans easily located the entrance shaft to the cave and dropped in explosives that killed ten officers and men of the staff. Despite all the casualties the 32nd Army had had since 1st April, these deaths on 21st June were the first battle losses the 32nd Army staff had sustained in the whole campaign.

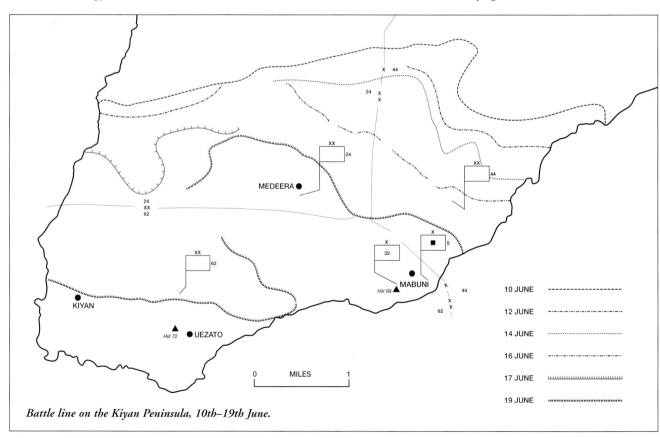

Battle line on the Kiyan Peninsula, 10th–19th June.

This meant that there were no longer any fighting units between the 32nd Army staff and its adversary. Even as late as 3rd June, when two-thirds of 32nd Army's strength had been lost, there had been almost no casualties at battalion level or above because line troops had sacrificed themselves to shield the staffs. As of 22nd June this had ceased to be the case. Nothing stood between the US 7th Infantry Division and the commanders of 32nd Army.

Since the 32nd Army had ceased to exist, planning its operations was a dead letter. Now the 32nd Army staff, which was all that remained of the original 100,000-man organisation, had to attend to the orderly dissolution of itself. This process had begun on 18th June with the round of farewell orders and messages. A banquet was also held on that day for the 32nd Army staff, marking the beginning of the end, even as shells were exploding on the ground overhead. The banquet was a farewell dinner, included tinned goods and sake, like that preceding the 4th May offensive. General Ushijima and his entire staff were there. It was not a gala, however. The best Scotch had not survived the retreat, and the headquarters itself was only a natural cave which had been a little improved, and where officers bumped their heads on stalactites and water dripped constantly.

With farewell orders and the obligatory banquet out of the way, headquarters staffs themselves began to think about 'honourable death attacks'. The various headquarters at the Mabuni command cave resolved on 21st June to 'stand to die in order'. In other words, brigade staffs, division staffs, then staffs of army headquarters units would conduct 'honourable death attacks' in sequence, followed finally by suicide of the 32nd Army commanders.

Formally exempted from this expectation were the young officers of the 32nd Army staff, however. From the beginning, Cho had maintained that the IJA had been crippled by the wanton self-destruction of staffs in the Pacific. Therefore, Cho decided, and ordered, that all of the staff officers of the 32nd Army would avoid honourable death and ritual suicide. He specified that Yahara, Miyake, Nagano, and others would report to IGHQ on the battle. Kimura, Kusumaru, and others would escape from the Kiyan Peninsula to north Okinawa and wage guerrilla warfare. Each staff member was therefore ordered to make his escape on the night of 19th June, and about 20 officers and escort troops did. Even so, some remained out of a sense of loyalty to their commanders.

An effort was also made to infiltrate ordinary soldiers through the American Marine and Army lines to carry on guerrilla warfare in the north. Troops sent north through the American lines travelled in groups of two or three, wore civilian clothes,

Above: *Two soldiers of the 32nd Regiment, 7th Infantry Division, look over the bodies of staff officers and aides of Lieutenant General Mitsuru Ushijima, Japanese commander of Okinawa. The bodies were found in a cave on Hill 89 in southern Okinawa, these officers having joined their general in suicide.*

and carried small arms only. A group usually carried only one firearm and some grenades. They moved on the night of 18th–19th June and on several nights following. The Americans, by this time accustomed to small-scale infiltration, put up illumination flares to detect these soldiers and killed most of them in the open.

However, most of the troops at Mabuni and Medeera were told by their officers to continue to resist where they were. The 32nd Army staff heard on 21st June that the 5th Artillery Command headquarters had made an 'honourable death attack' the preceding night. The headquarters staff of the 24th Division near Medeera still held out, but the 32nd Army staff had no way of knowing this, and the Americans would soon control all the entrances to the 32nd Army command cave at Mabuni.

It was resolved therefore that the officers and men still present at the headquarters on 21st June would attack the Americans that night and drive them off the crest of Hill 89, which overlooked the headquarters cave, about 400 yards away. On the night of 21st–22nd June, by moonlight, the headquarters guard unit charged up the steep slopes toward the Americans; this was their final act. At this same time, in the respite thus guaranteed Ushijima and Cho were to commit ritual suicide.

General Ushijima's cook described what happened. At about 22:00 on the night of 21st–22nd June, he was ordered to prepare an especially large dinner. He made it as sumptuous as he could, with rice, tinned meats, potatoes, fried fish cakes, salmon, fresh cabbage, pineapples, tea, and sake. While the generals ate this feast, the cook immediately began making breakfast, as was customary, since no cooking smoke could be exposed after daylight. This saved his life, as he would otherwise have been sent like almost everyone else, including the sentry at the cave entrance, to attack Hill 89 at 23:30.

From his kitchen near the cave mouth, the cook was able to witness the generals' ritual suicides later that night. At about 03:40, as the moon was just setting into the ocean, Ushijima and Cho went out of the cave onto the narrow ledges overlooking the sea. The ledges were too narrow for the generals to face north toward the imperial palace. Both Ushijima and Cho then committed seppuku, with their aides severing their heads instantly to minimise their suffering. Three orderlies secretly buried the bodies. Then, the remaining staff members obligingly went back into the cave to eat the breakfast the cook had prepared. That was the end of it. When night fell on 22nd June, the cook fled, and the remaining staff sortied in their final 'honourable death attack' against the Americans who were, by now, in dugouts less than 100 feet away.

Elements around the headquarters of the 24th Division at Medeera still fought on, but not for long. Only the 22nd Regiment remained, and the 24th Division headquarters lost contact with it on 23rd June. The 22nd Regiment was overrun soon after. Somehow, the 24th Division headquarters managed to survive until 30th June, when its members also committed suicide in their command cave just south of Medeera. This was an epilogue, however. Most observers describe the fighting as having effectively ended on 21st June.

Although the 32nd Army had ceased to exist, some of its members survived. Some lived passively but did not surrender, as Ito Koichi's men did in the same caves they had dug many months before. Also, remnants of the Kunigami Detachment were still in the mountains in the far north.

For the first time in the Pacific war, substantial numbers of IJA troops surrendered, 7,400 in all. Many, though, did not. Soldiers in the 32nd Army were reluctant to surrender for several reasons: they were ordered not to surrender, and it was

Japanese surrender
For the first time in the Pacific War, some Japanese troops surrendered rather than commit suicide or fight to the last man. More than 300 Japanese soldiers surrendered to the US Sixth Marine Division during the final 24-hours of organized resistance – the total figure was 7,400, although many of these were native Okinawans.

Above: *Japanese aviator on board a US ship.*

Right: *Here they crowd a prisoner of war stockade.*

Below right: *A disconsolate Japanese prisoner of war.*

Below: *A surrendering soldier, his head bandaged, emerges from a cave.*

customary not to, but above all, their officers had told them that they would be tortured and killed if captured.

Unfortunately, the prohibition against surrender left a large number of miserable and desperate IJA soldiers in open terrain. Sometimes, they committed suicide by stepping into a fire zone or by holding a grenade to their stomachs, a kind of 'poor man's seppuku'. Regrettably, during this period, many attacked the civilian population. There were many cases in the Pacific war where Japanese soldiers carried out atrocities against subject peoples. Here, the atrocities were committed on a large scale against Japanese citizens. Knowing that death was imminent, the soldiers freely committed rape. In some cases, fearing discovery, the soldiers forced parents to kill their crying babies, or the soldiers killed the infants themselves. Sometimes, they killed Okinawans seeking to share a cave, fearing they were spies. This widespread abuse left deep scars and, to this day, is a divisive influence between the people of metropolitan Japan and of Okinawa. For the average soldier, post battle suicide was neither voluntary nor dignified. The no-surrender policy for the mass of

soldiers was dehumanising and had the unintended consequence of victimising large numbers of Japanese civilians.

Japanese Casualties

IJA casualties in the Okinawa campaign are easy to calculate because there were only two kinds: prisoners of war or killed in action. The Japanese had 100,000 men on Okinawa, 67,000 IJA, 9,000 IJN, and 24,000 native Okinawans. Of these, 7,400 were taken prisoner and almost all the rest perished, the exception being the handful who surrendered after the war ended on 15th August. Many of the 7,400 captured were hastily impressed native Okinawans who were less imbued with the no-surrender spirit.

Some 70,000 Japanese soldiers were lost in the first eight weeks of fighting on the Okinawa isthmus. All of these were front line soldiers and company level officers, leaving only the 32nd Army's staffs and technical and rear-area personnel. The heavy artillery was still intact, but most of the infantry weapons were lost by the time of the 27th May – 3rd June retreat. The result after 3rd June was that non-combat soldiers often had to fight without weapons. These troops were simply overwhelmed. Whole lines melted away, and casualties in the third week of June skyrocketed, reaching 3,000 a day. For the first time on

Below: Excellent view of the invasion fleet with LCTs 1415, 1173, 1265 and 1049 on the beach, LSM-220 and LST-1000 further out.

Above: Most of the defenders of Okinawa died where they fought – nearly 93,000 native Okinawans, Imperial Japanese Army and Navy personnel died.

Okinawa, IJA soldiers went into the caves and cowered there for safety instead of using them as active fortifications.

For the first time, Americans were able to move from cave to cave with flamethrower tanks and explosives meeting little resistance between. American official histories tend to describe this easy advance as a matter of 'anti-cave' techniques being finally perfected, but the almost complete lack of weapons and training of the remaining Japanese soldiers may have been the main factor. The IJN stand on Oroku, in contrast, though it also involved people untrained in fighting, had extensive weaponry, especially machine guns, and thereby prevented an easy American advance. American sources do not make much of the Japanese lack of weapons on Kiyan; perhaps they considered that even one machine gun in Japanese hands was one too many.

Japanese officer observers all believed, however, that the shortage of small arms and anti-tank weapons was decisive for the poor quality of IJA fighting in the final weeks.

American Casualties

The secondary accounts of the Okinawa battle usually suggest that, against the Japanese combat losses of 100,000 dead or captured, the Americans suffered losses of only some 6,000 dead. This indicates a highly favourable American loss ratio of 1 to 17. But the overall impact of Okinawa on American personnel was less one-sided than these figures suggest. Only 76,000 men in the Japanese force were uniformed and trained military; the other 24,000 persons were recently impressed indigenous militia and labour units. Despite the IJA's periodic use of Okinawans in service roles, 76,000 is probably a more realistic figure for the force US divisions faced.

To subdue these 76,000 IJA regulars cost US Tenth Army exactly 6,319 killed in action between 1st April and 30th June 1945. This figure is still 8.3 per cent (1 in 12) of the Japanese number killed. What the figures conceal, however, is the substantial US losses in categories other than killed in action. The Tenth Army losses from 1st April to 30th June wounded and injured in action, missing, and died of wounds totalled 32,943, in addition to the 6,319 killed in action. Nor does the 6,319 figure include an additional 33,096 casualties in the 'non-battle' categories of sick, injured, other, and deaths. In other words, besides the killed in action, 66,039 Americans were lost to combat on account of wounds, illness, and death from various causes.

Some of these non-killed-in-action casualties may have involved minor injuries, allowing those concerned an early return to the fighting front. That such was not overwhelmingly the case is suggested by the strength reports of the fighting divisions. As of 8th April, the present-for-duty strength of the four infantry and two Marine divisions, plus XXIV Corps and III Amphibious Corps service personnel, was 146,451. Added to these units' strength from 1st April to 30th June was a small but steady flow of replacements that totalled 22,801 men. The original force plus the replacements totalled 169,252 men. Nevertheless, the present-for-duty strength of the six divisions and two corps on 30th June was 101,462. These figures show that 67,790 American soldiers were no longer with the units. Other than those killed in action 61,471 men were therefore still not capable of resuming their duties a week after the battle had ended. In other words, of the 66,039 non-killed-in-action casualties, 61,471 were still serious enough that they had not reappeared for duty after the battle.

It is likely that many of these 61,471 men would return to duty after weeks or months, after putting a proportionate strain on the medical system. Nevertheless, if all casualties are counted, not just the killed in action, the Americans' short and medium term loss from Okinawa operations totalled 72,358 men (6,319 killed, 32,943 wounded and other battle casualties, and 33,096 non battle casualties). In addition to this there has to added the US Navy losses in men and ships. It should be remembered that Admiral Nimitz was very concerned that 'losses of a ship and a half a day' were being sustained and the crews of the ships were under considerable pressure because of the kamikaze attacks. This total is not too different from the total of IJA regulars present. American planners' anxieties about invading Japan proper may have sprung from this fact, known to them but not emphasised later, that the US total casualty figure on Okinawa was 72,000 men.

Conclusion

The Japanese achievement on Okinawa was remarkable. Despite being outnumbered 2-to-1 in manpower and outgunned 10-to-1 in ground firepower alone, the Japanese mounted a dogged

defence for ten weeks, denied their adversary strategically desired terrain, and inflicted casualties in all categories almost equal to their own numbers. Okinawa was the only occasion in the Pacific war, apart from Iwo Jima, where an IJA force acquitted itself so well. The credit for this achievement must go in part to staff decisions made long before the battle began. The building of the fire-port caves and the development of the tactics for their use, as much as any other factors, allowed 32nd Army to offset the effect of the overwhelming land, air, and sea bombardment directed against it.

Although not usually thought of in these terms, the battle for Okinawa was a case where diligent staff work countered disproportionate firepower. Moreover, the Okinawa tactical solutions came mainly from the staff at the place where the battle was to be fought, and who had to implement them, They also had to ignore both the IJA's deeply ingrained traditions of light infantry attack and the specific directives they received from higher headquarters. The staff members of the 32nd Army were alone in their final responsibility for the outcome and also alone in the solutions they devised. Though none of the units present on Okinawa had served in earlier Pacific campaigns, the

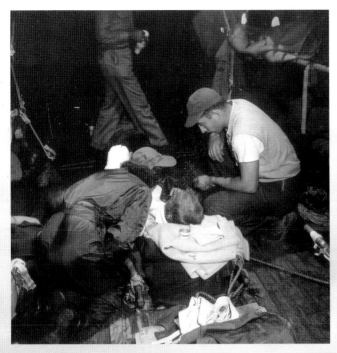

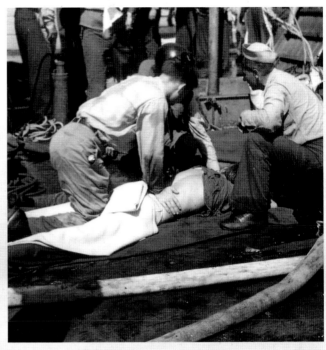

Inset, left: *Medics examine a wounded man on the first evacuation flight from Okinawa.*

Inset, right: *A crewman of the USS* Birmingham *(CL-62) is given artificial respiration by his shipmates. He had been extracted from a compartment that flooded as result of a kamikaze strike.*

Main photograph: LCI-1069 *tied up alongside the hospital ship USS* Comfort *(AH-6) off Okinawa.* Comfort *was commissioned on 5th May 1944 and operated with a Navy crew and Army medical personnel. She stood by off Okinawa 2nd–9th April, receiving wounded for evacuation to Guam. She returned to Okinawa on 23 April, and on the 29th she was struck by a Japanese kamikaze which killed 28 people (including six nurses), wounded 48 others and caused considerable damage.*

Okinawa staff did, to some extent, develop their tactics in the light of earlier combat experiences in the Pacific. Nonetheless, the 32nd Army staff members were successful iconoclasts who tempered their own operational education in defiance of what they were advised to do by faraway theoreticians.

The Okinawa battle was unusual in that it exhibited the stasis and lethality of World War I fronts even though it employed the full range of mobile World War II weapons: tanks, aircraft, radios, and trucks. On Okinawa, the modern weapons increased battle zone lethality due to bombardment and fire, without doing anything to decrease the static quality of the front. This suggests that dense battle, the 'fire-swept zone' characteristic of World War I, may occur in modern warfare regardless of weaponry, wherever two large forces are concentrated to acquire the same finite objective. Episodes of dense battle therefore took place in World War II on Okinawa and Iwo Jima, as well as in the urban siege warfare of the several European fronts.

Dense battle makes special demands of an infantry force. Infantry on the surface in the fire-swept zone, whether attacking or counter-attacking, must be fearless, agile, technically ingenious, and tolerant of heavy casualties. World War I staff officers invented a new kind of soldier that exemplified these qualities, the storm troops. Paradoxically, the old IJA doctrine's emphasis on fearless, almost thoughtless, light infantry attack was a suitable preparation for surface combat in the fire-swept zone. Light infantry combat, even hand-to-hand combat, flourished at the margins of the fire-swept zone, and in dense

battle everything is done by margins. The IJA's old tactics of boldness, small-unit initiative, self-sacrifice, and close fighting were, unintentionally, an ideal training for dense battle in counter-attack warfare, even though that training was contrary to the larger operational tactics needed on Okinawa.

The Okinawa infantry fighting, besides taking place in an environment of unusually high lethality, consisted on both sides of a main weapon, in caves or tanks, and the rifle teams protecting them. This pattern, the use of machine guns or machine-gun strongpoints, also emerged in the no-man's-land fighting of World War I. The Okinawa experience suggests that this tactical grouping may be one of the most basic in modern combat and likely to appear in a wide variety of circumstances and regardless of the specific configuration of the weapon. This means a modern operational planner must pay attention to both elements of the equation, the skilled infantry team and the main weapon. On Okinawa, the US Tenth Army won with tanks, and the IJA 32nd Army defended as long as it did with sited fire ports that were low in technology but high in sophistication. Even so, both the caves and tanks were vulnerable unless protected by infantry, who ended in duelling at close ranges with small arms to decide the outcome.

Besides providing insights into modern infantry tactics, the Okinawa campaign demonstrates the transformation in defensive fortifications ordained by air power. The World War I trench erected a barrier toward the enemy in the front. But the advent of aircraft required a barrier against the enemy above. On

Above: Marine casualties are rushed from ambulance jeep to an awaiting Grasshopper for speedy evacuation to a hospital.

Right: Casualties arriving from USS McDermut *(DD-677) are* transferred aboard USS Wisconsin *(BB-64).*

Left: Marines placing wounded in an LVT-4 Amtrac while Japanese troops are flushed out from the sea wall on West Beach.

Okinawa, the entire Japanese Army moved underground, lived underground, and performed most combat functions underground. This arrangement may prove a necessary feature of any future combat effort that does not enjoy air superiority. The IJA's operations on Okinawa offer some helpful clues with respect to the effective use of such underground forts.

Finally, Japan's Okinawa experience demonstrates what resourceful and determined soldiers can do, even when facing superior numbers and simultaneous overwhelming lethality on land, air, and sea. Intelligence and diligence can stand against even the most extreme technological superiority. But not forever. Ultimately, brave men and overwhelming firepower will always defeat brave men alone.

CHAPTER 6 Cave Warfare on Okinawa

by Dale E. Floyd

By the fall of 1944, the United States was in the final phase of its war against the Empire of Japan. The ultimate goal of American operations in the Pacific was the industrial heart of Japan, the south coast of Honshu. Throughout most of 1944, the Americans planned an invasion of Formosa, Operation Causeway, to support the attack on the Japanese home islands. When General Douglas MacArthur, Commander in Chief, Southwest Pacific Area, attacked Leyte in October rather than December, Admiral Chester Nimitz, Commander in Chief, Pacific Ocean Area, felt that the possibility of an early advance into the central Philippines opened a direct approach route north through the Ryukyus rather than by way of Formosa.

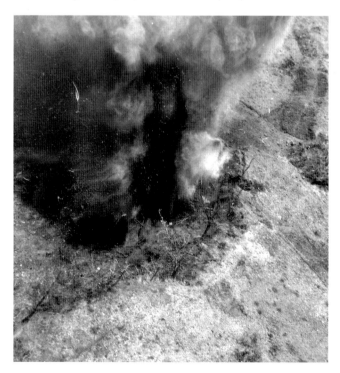

Thus was born Operation Iceberg, the attack on the largest of the Ryukyu Islands, Okinawa. The island was within medium bomber range of Japan and, with airfield construction, could sustain a force of 780 bombers. Good fleet anchorages were available in the Okinawa island group, and from these air and naval bases the Americans could attack the Japanese Home Islands and support the invasion of Kyushu and finally Honshu.

Okinawa is 69 miles long and from 2 to 18 miles wide, comprising a total area of 485 square miles. With a subtropical climate, Okinawa's temperatures range from 60°F to 83°F, and high humidity makes it oppressive during the rainy season from May to November. This rough, generally mountainous coral island has two types of terrain. The northern part, roughly two-thirds of the island, is generally rocky with a high ridge running its length covered with forests and heavy undergrowth. The southern one-third of the island, where most of the people live and practically all cultivation occurs, comprises rolling hills dotted with deep ravines and sharp limestone ridges.

American knowledge of the terrain and enemy situation was acquired over a period of months and with some difficulty. While limited information was gathered from old publications and captured documents, the bulk of the data came from aerial photos. The engineers constructed models of particular objectives based on intelligence and reconnaissance work, including a highly accurate one of the Mount Shuri/Shuri Castle area, that would be the most heavily defended real estate in Okinawa. With

Left: Aerial of terrain near Love Hill north of Yonaburu. The ridge from lower left to upper right divided opposing troops from the Japanese troops.

Right: Marines dig out Japanese during mopping up operations on Saipan in Mariana Islands.

cloud cover hindering full coverage, the 1:25,000 scale target map had incomplete detail, especially in the south.

It was in the south that Lieutenant-General Ushijima Mitsuru, Japanese 32nd Army commander, decided to make his stand. As a beach defence would subject his troops to murderous American naval gunfire and a defence in the north would not deprive the Americans of the airfields and harbours of the south, Ushijima determined that the best use of the force available to him was a defence of southern Okinawa.

Southern Okinawa, south of Kuba on the east coast, was ideally suited for defence. The soft limestone ridges included numerous caves with natural cover and concealment. The Okinawans had converted some of the caves into burial tombs.

The Japanese, already known as tenacious fighters, would maximise their capabilities by establishing a strong point-defence strategy using cave warfare. Lieutenant-General Cho Isamu, Ushijima's chief of staff, who was one of Japan's foremost experts on point defence, took overall charge of the defensive operations. Japanese unit commanders from brigade to company level determined the location and design of defences in their own sector while subordinates oversaw actual construction at particular sites. Reserve units set up anti-aircraft defences.

In August 1944, the Japanese began in earnest to construct their defences. Besides their own men, commanders used Okinawa home guards, called Boeitai; attached labour personnel; and local village conscripts, including school children, to do the work. In adapting the defence to the terrain, the Japanese built blockhouses and pillboxes into the hills and fortified the natural caves, even the tombs.

Some of the hundreds of fortified caves were more than one-storey high. Practically every cave had multiple exits and tunnels connecting to other caves. For the first time in the Pacific War, the Japanese had adequate artillery and mortars that they thoroughly integrated into the defences. The size of cave exits varied but most were small, even as little as two feet square, partly to escape detection but also because they doubled as weapons embrasures and to provide as little space as possible for the entry of enemy artillery shells.

Although the Japanese generally lacked concrete and steel for cave lining, some steel was available for covering entrances. Logs often shored up the caves. Once inside the small entrances, the caves opened up into larger spaces, often comprising more than one room. Some caves had separate rooms for various purposes including barracks, mess, ammunition storage, and radio transmission.

The main defensive positions were on the reverse slopes. All of the defences, including the ordnance, were cleverly camouflaged. After the construction work ceased, the Japanese placed mines and booby traps in their defences.

Left: An American flamethrowing tank bursts into action against the cave defences which honeycomb the rocky ridges of Okinawa. With the help of the rugged and difficult terrain, the Japanese stubbornly contested possession of the strategic island. By 9th May US forces were within a mile of the capital city of Naha, and US naval guns were shelling the formidable line of Japanese fortifications protecting the city.

Below: A demolition crew from the 6th Marine Division watches dynamite charges explode and destroy a Japanese cave.

Above: US soldiers (circled) run for cover as their white phosphorus charge explodes at the mouth of a cave.

Right: Three Marines of the 6th Division take a short pause in the day's operations to smoke out Japanese troops who might have been hiding in the hole behind the jagged coral boulder (right center). The camera caught the flash of the exploding smoke grenade during the one-day operation against Senega Shima, small rocky islet just off the coast of Okinawa.

Although few enemy minefields existed, the Americans did discover effective ones at crucial tank approach points such as road junctions, turn-offs, and defiles. The Japanese used a newly developed mine on Okinawa, an anti-personnel fragmentation mine that the rocky terrain made difficult to detect. They also dug ditches and created tank traps covered by supporting fire. From the time an American tank entered an avenue of approach, it was under constant attack from direct and indirect fire.

Manning the defences was the Japanese 32nd Army. Its infantry strength consisted of the 62nd and 24th Divisions, the 44th Independent Mixed Brigade, and some converted naval units. A tank regiment, four machine-gun battalions, and various artillery units supplemented the divisional forces. The

artillerymen, veterans of several campaigns, were considered among the best in the Japanese Army. Conscripted Okinawans and the Boeitai were forced to serve with the army. At the time of the American attack, the 32nd Army strength was over 100,000 men.

On 1st April 1945, Easter Sunday and April Fool's Day, the American Tenth Army assaulted the island of Okinawa. The Tenth Army consisted of two corps: the XXIV Corps had three Army divisions, the 7th, 77th, and 96th, and the III Amphibious Corps had three Marine divisions, the 1st, 2nd, and 6th. Operation Iceberg required an attack directly across the island to capture the two airfields and split the enemy force. Then, while the Marines held in the north, XXIV Corps

would attack and overrun Japanese defences in the south. Once that was accomplished, they would attack the Japanese forces in the north.

The Japanese expected the Americans to use the good west coast beaches and immediately strike out for the nearby airfields, Yontan and Kadena. A week before, the American 77th Division had seized the Kerama Islands as a fleet anchorage and the Keise Islands as an offshore artillery platform for the Okinawa beach assault. Thus, the Japanese did not defend the beaches and the Americans quickly seized the two airfields and cut the island in half. By 3rd April, it was clear to Lieutenant General Simon B. Buckner, Jr., Commanding General, Tenth Army, that there were few Japanese in the north. In a change of plans, he sent the

Marines there while at the same time he pushed the XXIV Corps south toward the main Japanese defences.

While the Japanese high command was determined to hold Okinawa, General Ushijima was more realistic and decided that the best he could do was to hold out for as long as possible and inflict maximum casualties. He made his stand on strongly fortified, concentric defence lines constructed in the south around the Shuri Heights high ground. In accordance with Japanese defence doctrine, each position protected its own location as well as an adjacent one; the key was mutual support through coordinated fire.

The 96th Infantry Division had reached the first Japanese defence line, Kakazu Ridge, by 8th April. The next day, in a

surprise attack without artillery support, the 383rd Infantry Regiment made a frontal assault. It seized the forward slope and reached but could not hold the ridge line. The reverse slope defence system of pillboxes, tunnels, and caves with machine guns, mortars, and artillery covering all avenues of approach was too strong for a direct infantry attack. This attack taught the Americans that the key to success was an attack on the reverse slope defences while a large force engaged and prevented the forward slope defenders from providing any support.

The next attack on the Kakazu Ridge line was corps-size with the 7th and 27th Divisions added to the 96th. From 18th to 24th April, these XXIV Corps units supported by 29 artillery battalions plus air strikes and naval gunfire fought the Japanese along this initial defence line. The 102nd Engineer Combat Battalion built a foot bridge, two Bailey bridges, and a pontoon bridge to place the 27th Division in position for an attack. The 7th Division, even though supported by the first use of armoured flamethrowers of the 713th Tank Battalion, was unable to dislodge the Japanese from reverse slope positions along Skyline Ridge. By 20th April, only the 27th Division was in position to attack into the rear of the Japanese defence line; the 7th and 96th Divisions would have to continue the frontal attacks.

The rear of the Kakazu Ridge was the 27th Division's target. The 102nd Engineers sealed Japanese caves along the forward slopes of the Pinnacles, depriving the reverse slope defenders of covering fire. On 24th April, the Japanese began an orderly withdrawal from the outer Shuri defence as their line was penetrated and the strongpoints battered.

American veterans of the Pacific war recognised the techniques and tactics of the Japanese defence: intricate and elaborate underground positions, and full use of cover and concealment soundly based on a reverse slope concept. They had experienced it all the way from Guadalcanal to Leyte. But on Okinawa, the Japanese used all their experience to produce the strongest defence the Americans confronted in the Pacific war.

As the Americans reviewed the campaign, they realised that the enormous amounts of heavy explosives used did deny the Japanese freedom of movement above ground but did not have much of an effect on underground positions. Something else was needed, and the solution proved to be the tank–infantry team supported by armoured flamethrowers, artillery, and engineer demolition squads. The tactics involved a highly coordinated

effort by all members of the team. As the artillery battered a position to force the defenders back into a tunnel, tanks took up direct fire positions while the infantry protected the tanks from Japanese infantry attack. flamethrower tanks were used to destroy many positions, but where the terrain was not suitable for armour, the engineers used a portable flamethrower with a range of 40 yards.

The need to destroy Japanese positions completely to preclude their reuse, and the heavy infantry casualties, made the use of engineers in demolition squads necessary. An engineer squad of 6–12 men assisted infantry units up to battalion size and usually camped near the infantry headquarters to be readily available.

The demolition squad's initial responsibility was to clear the area of mines as the tank–infantry team approached the objective. Upon nearing the target, one engineer with a charge and a phosphorus grenade took the lead while several others followed with spare satchels, the usual weapon employed by the demolition squads. A standard charge weighing 24 pounds was fused by an engineer using a special blasting cap and had either a waterproof fuse lighter or a 15-second delay igniter. While the infantry provided covering fire, the lead engineer threw the phosphorus grenade into the cave to blind the defenders and then, to gain maximum effect, delivered the satchel charge as far as possible into the position.

For large positions, the engineers often resorted to pumping petrol from trucks into the openings and igniting it with tracer bullets or phosphorus grenades; the 13th Engineers, 7th Division, used a 1,000-gallon water distributer and 200–300 feet of hose to pump petrol into caves. In a three-week period, the 77th Division's 302nd Engineer Combat Battalion (ECB) destroyed 925 Japanese defensive works using an average of 3,500 pounds of explosives per day. The 302nd Battalion expended a total of 65 tons of explosives during the entire campaign on Okinawa and the nearby islands. General Buckner called this the 'blowtorch and corkscrew' method; the blowtorch was the liquid flame and the corkscrew was the explosive.

When possible, the demolition squad obtained a foothold above a cave opening and attacked down the hill in what were termed 'straddle attacks'. This method denied the defenders direct fire against the attackers. In all instances, mutual supporting defensive fire had to be silenced before the demolition squads could go into action. The tanks and infantry waged the battle, but frequently it was the flame and demolition squads that destroyed the position.

The Tenth Army included all of these attack methods in the tactics of an Army-size assault on the Shuri defence system.

Left: Bazookas were great bunker-busters. Here a Marine bazooka team sights on a target.

Since the northern operations were over, the Marines and the 77th Division came south. Then, with the III Amphibious Corps on the right and the XXIV Corps on the left, the Tenth Army planned an attack to double-envelop the final Shuri line.

As the Americans were getting into position, the Japanese counter-attacked on 4th May. When General Ushijima realised that the Americans were not going to conduct an amphibious operation in the south, he moved the 44th Independent Mixed Brigade and the 24th Division into the Shuri area. With that additional strength, he chanced an attack to try to push the Americans off the island. By 8th May, he knew he had failed, and on 11th May, the Americans resumed the offensive.

In the centre of the line, the 77th Division and the 1st Marine Division had slow going in frontal assaults on strong Japanese positions. The 77th Division brought all available fire to bear on limited objectives, seized forward slopes to clear reverse slope covering fire, and expended huge amounts of petrol and napalm to seal Japanese defensive positions as it fought south along Route 5 through hills given American names such as Chocolate Drop and Flattop. The 1st Marine Division attacked the Shuri Heights and, in spite of the fortified caves, made steady progress by concentrating on one specific objective at a time. The Marines called it 'processing'. By 21st May, both divisions were ready to break into the final Shuri position.

The enemy flanks were now the key to success for the Americans. On the right, the 6th Marine Division had a difficult fight taking two flanking hills before they could get tanks into the rear of Sugar Loaf Hill and reduce the Japanese reverse slope positions. The seizure of Sugar Loaf opened the way into the rear of the Shuri defences from the right. When the 96th Division took Conical Hill on the left flank, the Shuri rear area was open to attack. By 21st May, the possibility of a double envelopment of Shuri existed. Then the rains came.

General Ushijima knew his position was untenable so, under cover of the rain, he began his withdrawal from the Shuri defence system on 22nd May. By 31st May, the Americans had occupied Shuri, but the Japanese made good the escape of some of their force to a final defence position on the southern tip of the island.

The Americans continued the drive south and by 9th June were in position to attack the final Japanese defences, the Yaeju-Dake escarpment. The terrain there was good for armour. The tank–infantry teams and the demolition squads were more experienced and the Japanese artillery was depleted. But some of the largest cave defensive positions were in the area. It took the Americans three weeks to reduce the Yaeju-Dake area. No wonder that in one month of fighting on Okinawa, the combat

engineers in the three regimental zones destroyed 1,000 Japanese caves, pillboxes, bunkers, and defensive positions. Organised resistance was declared over on 21st June.

The Okinawa campaign proved to be expensive in men and materiel. In the final days, four general officers were killed. On 18th June, General Buckner was killed by artillery fire, and the next day Brigadier General Claudius M. Easley, assistant commander of the 96th Division, was killed by machine-gun fire. On 22nd June, Lieutenant-Generals Ushijima and Cho committed suicide.

On 23rd June American divisions formed a skirmish line across the island and began moving south in a final mop-up. The

Army either dug out or sealed the remaining Japanese in caves, pillboxes, and tombs. On 26th June, the 321st Engineer Combat Battalion of the 96th Division used 1,700 gallons of petrol and 300 pounds of dynamite to seal a cave which reportedly served as the headquarters of the Japanese 24th Division. Finally, on 2nd July 1945, Lieutenant-General Joseph W. Stilwell, the new commander of the Tenth Army, declared the Okinawa campaign over.

On Okinawa, the engineers played a major combat role in addition to their normal supply and construction duties. Some engineer units had significant losses: the 302nd Engineer Combat Battalion sustained 20 per cent casualties in one three-

Above: Weapons at the ready, Marines await the result of an explosive charge in an cave to pick off any Japanese who attempt to escape. These caves formed the Japanese 'Little Siegfried Line', defending the capital city of Naha.

week period. Of the total force on Okinawa when the fighting ended, approximately 31,400, or 18.6 per cent, were engineer troops. The victory on Okinawa was made possible by the combat accomplishments of the engineers.

CHAPTER 7 US Naval Losses and the Invasion of Japan

by Lowry Cole

For the US Navy the Okinawa campaign began on 14th March when Task Force 58, the main striking force of the US Pacific Fleet, commenced operations against airfields on Kyushu. The first ship was hit on 17th February, and from then until 30th July when the last ship was hit in the campaign 162 vessels were damaged by enemy action. Of these, 35 were sunk or scuttled, 27 were so badly damaged as to be not worth repairing, and 41 had not had their damage repaired before the war ended. There were at least 2,000 kamikaze attacks on the invasion fleet during the campaign, which inflicted 475 direct hits or near misses that damaged the target vessels. Of the ships sunk most were destroyers and light craft, but battleships, fleet and escort carriers and cruisers were also hit. In some cases these larger vessels were damaged so severely that they were no longer able to operate and had to be withdrawn for repairs to be effected. In total 4,907 members of the crews of the ships were killed and 4,824 were wounded. Figures are not available for 'non battle casualties' such as those resulting from illness, injuries, or psychiatric and other problems brought on by the strain of the continuous fighting – and the number of these could have been substantial.

Admiral Spruance, the commander of the 5th Fleet and the commander of the operation, had his first flag ship, the cruiser Indianapolis so badly damaged on the first day of the invasion that he had to move his flag to the battleship New Mexico. On 12th May the New Mexico was hit by a kamikaze which killed and wounded 50 men. Spruance remained on the ship until his relief by Admiral Halsey on 27th May. Admiral Nimitz, the Commander-in-Chief of the Pacific Fleet and Pacific Ocean Area, was so concerned at the continuing loss of ships that during his visit to the battle front on 23rd April he told General Buckner, his Army commander, that the ground operations were not proceeding fast enough. Buckner's response was that it was a ground operation, the implication being that the fighting on the island was none of the Navy's business. Nimitz's response was 'Yes, but ground though it may be, I'm losing a ship and a half a day. So if the line [meaning the front line] isn't moving within five days, we'll get someone here to move it so we can all get out from under these stupid air attacks.'

The ships of the invasion force were under continuous attack throughout the entire operation; the crews were under constant threat, with action alarms and gunfire ensuring that no one could relax. The US Fifth Air Force's attacks on Formosa were unable to destroy the enemy aircraft which had been widely dispersed on the island.

Main photograph: *Fighting fires caused by a kamikaze strike on USS Intrepid (CV-11).*

Below: *Funeral services held aboard USS Hancock (CV-19) for 28 victims killed in the 7th April kamikaze attack.*

The impact of these losses was such that Admiral King, the US Chief of Naval Operations came to the conclusion that an invasion of Japan was not practical. King came to this conclusion for a number of reasons, which included the lessons learnt from the Okinawa campaign, in particular the casualties suffered and the shipping loss. He knew that the Japanese forces on Kyushu had grown to over half a million strong by early 194, and that by the time the invasion was to take place in November 1945 the number would be considerably greater. Signals intelligence indicated that by August 1945 there were 14 divisions on Kyushu and with other IJA units it was estimated there were 625,000 soldiers. This figure, it turned out, was an underestimate; there were in fact 900,000 soldiers on the island. Comparing these figures with those of the Okinawa campaign implied a US casualty figure of over half a million, and if the lessons of Okinawa were fully learned by the Japanese the total casualties might well be in the region of a million. To this must be added the shipping losses. Obviously these would be far higher than at Okinawa, as the US fleet would be under continuous kamikaze attack.

The Japanese plan was to make an all-out assault with all types of kamikaze weapons on the invasion fleet. All the kamikaze air units were to be used, and none were to be held back for later battles. The number of aircraft assigned to the kamikaze units was in the region of 5,300; in addition there were at least a further

5,000 available that had not been assigned to the suicide units. In addition there were also over 7,000 damaged aircraft which, if repaired, could be added to these totals. The IJA planned to launch kamikaze attacks in waves of 300 to 400 aircraft at hourly intervals. The IJA expected the IJN to carry out similar attacks. This would have meant that the invasion fleet would have faced in a single day a kamikaze attack greater than was faced over a three-month period at Okinawa. The IJA and IJN had also been training the kamikaze air crews to attack the troop transports and cargo vessels rather than the far better protected warships.

The US Navy's analysis of kamikaze attacks up to the end of the Okinawa campaign had shown that shells from 20mm and 40mm anti-aircraft guns would not necessarily stop a kamikaze aircraft; this required the firepower of 5-inch guns with shells equipped with the VT (proximity) fuse. The troop transport and cargo vessels were equipped with both 20mm and 40mm guns, and some had one or two 5-inch weapons. Effectively they would have been defenceless against the kamikaze. But this was not all, there would have been attacks by suicide boats, including submarines with two torpedoes, manned torpedoes and single-man motor boats – by the time of the Japanese surrender there were over 6,000 of this particular type in existence. Finally the IJN was training a 'Water's Edge Surprise Attack Force'. This consisted of individuals wearing diving suits who would station themselves in shallow waters off the landing beaches; they were to thrust themselves against landing craft, destroying them (and themselves) in the resultant explosion.

Each US Army division was to have an additional regiment as part of its establishment for the assault on Japan. This was to permit regular rotation out of the front line. However, the US Army's manpower problems were very considerable. After the German surrender it had been decided to discharge large numbers of soldiers from the Army. First of all it was considered that far fewer troops would be necessary for the attack on Japan than had been required to defeat Germany, secondly there was enormous pressure, particularly political, for the return home for discharge of those troops who had served the longest in the European Theatre of Operations. This resulted in US Army units no longer being battle ready. This meant that the replacements had to be trained and absorbed into the units that were to be used for the battle of Japan, and there were doubts that the US Army would have sufficient manpower available for the forthcoming battle.

Admiral King was aware of these problems, and he became increasing unenthusiastic for the invasion to take place; by the time of the dropping of the atomic bombs on Japan he was taking active steps to ensure that it did not.

Left: *A Japanese kamikaze attack on USS* Columbia *(CL-56) in Lingayen Gulf, Philippine Islands.*

Below: *A machine gun from a Japanese kamikaze was ripped from its mounting and driven into muzzle of one of the 40mm anti-aircraft guns aboard the USS* Missouri *(BB-63).*

Kamikaze – 1

Over 2,000 attacks were made on the Allied fleet at Okinawa and their intensity led to substantial casualties and an incredible strain on resources. The first Kamikaze unit was formed on 20th October 1944 at Luzon to attack the Allied naval forces off Leyte. The first ship to be hit was the Australian cruiser Australia, which lost 20 men including its captain and was put out of action. She would be hit by five more kamikazes during the assault on Luzon. Many Allied ships took hits, the aircraft carriers being the main targets. Improved anti-kamikaze tactics, destruction of Japanese airfields by bombing and the inevitable difficulties of finding sufficient aircraft and pilots to undertake the missions would reduce the number and effectiveness of the attacks, but there is no doubt that an amphibious assault on Japan itself would have unleashed a huge wave of kamikazes.

Left: The USS Wilkes Barre (CL-103) fighting fires on USS Bunker Hill (CV-17).

Below left: USS Bunker Hill burns after being hit by a kamikaze.

Below right: USS Franklin (CV-13) lists after being hit by a kamikaze off Kyushu, Japan.

Opposite, above: Japanese 'Kate' (Nakajima B5N) kamikaze makes a suicide attack on the USS Texas (BB-35) during the Ie Jima landings.

Opposite below left: Kamikaze attack USS Missouri (BB-63).

Opposite, below right: Two attacks on USS Intrepid (CV-11); one explodes in sheet of flame on deck at same time its bomb explodes amidships, while the other plane explodes nearby.

Kamikaze – 2

The wooden decks of the US aircraft carriers meant that the damage caused by kamikaze aircraft was major. British carriers – there were four at Okinawa, Indefatigable, Indomitable, Illustrious and Victorious – were also hit by kamikazes but their armoured flight decks restricted the damage and they remained operational throughout.
.

Main photograph: *The USS* Enterprise *(CV-6) is hit by a Japanese aircraft during aerial attack on Task Group 58.3. The black object blown from* Enterprise *is one of the lifts that took aircraft from the hangar to the flight deck.*

Inset, above: *Fire damage on the flight deck of USS* Enterprise.

Inset, centre: *USS* Intrepid *(CV-11) hit by Japanese kamikaze.*

Inset, bottom: *Hospital ship and destroyer alongside USS* Enterprise *to remove casualties.*

Kamikaze – 3
The Japanese had plans to defend their homeland with waves of kamikazes – aircraft, midget submarines and ships. The three photos on this page show some of these different projects.

Main photograph: The Yokosuka Ohka (Cherry Blossom) was codenamed 'Baka' (Fool) by the Allies. It was built in various forms: as a training glider; as the Model 11, the main production version, of which 755 were built; the 22, which was smaller; the 33, designed to be carried by the Renzan bomber; and the 43 that was designed to be fired from catapults. The Model 11 was carried by the Mitsubishi G4M 'Betty' bomber. A number were found on Okinawa.

Inset, above: Two-man kamikaze midget submarines on Yokosuka Naval Base, Japan.

Inset, centre: An Ohka on Okinawa.

Inset, below: Captured during the battle for the Kerama Islands, these suicide boats could achieve 32 knots.

Chapter 8 Prisoner of War Interrogation Reports

Colonel Yahara and Mr Shimada were captured soon after the end of the fighting on Okinawa. Colonel Yahara, together with a number of other staff officers of the 32nd Army's headquarters, had been ordered by Lt-General Cho not to kill themselves but to escape so that they could provide the benefit of their experiences of the Okinawa campaign to the IGHQ in Japan.

After Generals Ushijima and Cho had committed suicide on 23rd June, Yahara left the headquarters cave, dressed himself in civilian clothing and managed gradually to make his way northwards. In mid-July, whilst still on Okinawa, he was recognised and became a prisoner of war.

The capture of Colonel Yahara was most unusual. Japanese military personnel were not in the habit of surrendering, particularly officers, and, even more so, senior officers such as Yahara. But like so many of the Japanese who did surrender, he seems to have talked freely to his captors, though not about anything that he considered would compromise the defence of the homeland. This seems to have been naive. Yahara represented the brain of the Japanese Army. By discussing with the enemy how a campaign had been fought he provided a first hand insight into the battles that might have to be be fought during the conquest of Japan itself.

After serving briefly in the Army and being commissioned Mr Shimada worked in civilian occupations for six years. In 1939, using his friendship with General Cho, he joined the *Tokumu Kikan*. This shadowy secret organisation operated all over the world. Shimada served in China in the Peking and Taton (Daido) offices. In 1941 he obtained a discharge, on what seems to have been spurious medical grounds, and returned to civilian life. In 1943 he moved to Okinawa to run the theatre in Naha. In March 1945 he became General Cho's secretary. He was, therefore, in a unique position to witness the activities of the command group of the 32nd Army throughout the

campaign. Unlike Yahara he seems to have discussed not only the campaign but also the *Tokumu Kikan* with his interrogators. In addition he talked about the construction of fortifications in Japan which he had seen during his last visit to the homeland in late 1944. Other sources also indicate he had connections to the Yakuza, the Japanese criminal underworld. This would not have been unusual as the Yakuza had worked closely with the military extremists, assisting with murders and blackmail when required.

The 'reports' that follow have been set in a different style of type. Throughout the reports American forces were originally referred to as 'Blue'; this term has been replaced by 'US'. Explanatory comments appear in brackets [ ]. Some comments which were originally added by the interrogating officer appear with the prefix IN.

Below: A Marine dashes through Japanese machine gun fire while crossing a draw, called 'Death Valley' by the men fighting there. Marines sustained more than 125 casualties in eight hours crossing this obstacle.

Below left: Tank-borne infantry of the 29th Marines moving up to take the town of Ghuta on Okinawa.

COLONEL YAHARA, HIROMICHI
Senior Staff Officer, 32nd Army, Age: 42
Captured: 15th July 1945 at Yabiku Civilian Compound

ASSESSMENT

1. Details of Capture
After attending the dinner preceding the suicides of Generals Ushijima and Cho, Yahara, in civilian clothes proceeded to carry out orders received from General Cho

'After participating in the final defence of Okinawa Island, Staff Officer Yahara will proceed and take part in the defence of the homeland.'

He made his escape from the Mabuni caves in a spectacular fashion, rolling over a cliff when observed by US troops, inadvertently firing his pistol during the descent. This performance was apparently the basis of the rumours that Yahara had been killed at Mabuni.

Alive, though bruised by the fall, Colonel Yahara joined a group of civilians in a cave, intending to remain with them and to work his way north, hoping eventually to reach Japanese Territory by small boat. When US troops approached the cave Yahara led the group out and accompanied them to the Yabiku compound where he successfully assumed the guise of a school teacher. Three days on a labour detail depleted Yahara's already

weakened endurance; he collapsed and spent the next two weeks resting. The presence of an idle but complaining stranger aroused the suspicion and resentment of an alert Okinawan who took Yahara aside and demanded an explanation. Yahara revealed his identity but appealed to the man's patriotism and begged his silence. To his chagrin the Okinawan immediately reported his presence to local CIC [Counter Intelligence Corps] agents who returned and took Yahara, bitter but unresisting, into custody.

2. Evaluation
Quiet and unassuming, yet possessed of a keen mind and fine discernment, Colonel Yahara is, from all reports, an eminently capable officer, described by some prisoners of war as the 'brains' of the 32nd Army.

His life falls in to the pattern of many career officers of the Japanese services. The son of a small country land-owner, Yahara won an appointment to the JMA, graduating in 1923. Although promotions came slowly he won some distinction as a junior officer and attended the War College, graduating, according to his account, fifth in his class (prisoners of war attribute this to negative modesty, holding that Yahara led his class). His subsequent assignments included duty in the United States, in China, and as a plain clothes agent in Siam, Burma and Malaya.

Colonel Yahara attributes his frequent change of duty to a propensity to disagree with superior officers which made him an undesirable among certain old-line officers.

Colonel Yahara discussed the Okinawa operation freely though he has indicated that he will not divulge information that he considers vital to the security of the Empire. There is no reason to believe that he made any attempt at deception. It should be borne in mind that his observation of the campaign was made from the comparative safety of Shuri castle and that in some instances his narrative may differ from that of front-line troops.

The present report deals only with the Okinawa operation, making no attempt to delve into the colonel's pre-Okinawan experiences.

3. Intelligence

a. Chronology

1923   Graduated from JMA. To 54th Infantry Regiment (Okayama).

1925   To 63rd Infantry Regiment.

1926   Entered Army War College.

1929   Graduated from War College. To 63rd Infantry Regiment.

1930   To Personnel Department of the War Ministry.

1933   To USA as an exchange officer. Wilmington, Boston, Washington D.C. With US 8th Infantry Regiment for six months at Fort Moultrie.

1935   Returned to Personnel Department, War Ministry.

1937   Appointed as instructor, strategy and tactics, at Army War College. Three months in China as staff officer with 2nd Army – North China Expeditionary Force.

1938   Returned to War College as instructor.

1940   September: As Japanese agent in Siam, Burma and Malaya
November: To General Staff as expert on S.E. Asia.

1941   July: To Bangkok as Assistant Military Attache.
November: Received secret orders to staff of 15th Army (Saigon).
Remained in Bangkok and participated in the negotiations for the peaceful occupation of Siam. Later participated in the Burma operation with 15th Army. Became ill and returned to Japan. Assigned again to War College as instructor.

1944   March: To Okinawa as advisor from IGHQ. 32nd Army Headquarters formed and assigned as Senior Staff Officer.

1945   July: Captured.

b. Pre L-Day Estimates and Preparations.

The successful US invasion of the Marianas convinced staff officers both in the 32nd Army and the General Staff that the US would attempt a landing either on Taiwan the Ryukyu Retto, or Hong Kong within the year. The 32nd Army staff believed that, because of its strategic position, Okinawa would certainly be invaded; opinion in Tokyo remained more indefinite, some favouring Taiwan. The attack was expected either as:

(a) An immediate landing based from and using troops available in the Marianas;

or

(b) An attack mounted from the South West Pacific Area when the tactical situation should permit the withdrawal of troops from that area.

The first possibility was regarded as a more dangerous threat since Okinawa was totally unprepared to repulse enemy landings at that time. The landings on the Palaus and on Leyte came as a respite, indicating that US plans did not include an immediate attack in this area. The landing was then expected from late March to June 1945, on the assumption that the situation in the Philippines would have eased sufficiently by that time to permit the withdrawal of troops and the use of Leyte as a staging area. The Okinawa landing was expected to take place before the Iwo Jima landing because Iwo Jima was considered of lesser importance. Some false confidence was inspired by intelligence reports that not enough troops were available to effect a landing on Okinawa for some time to come. However, in late February reports of shipping concentrations in the Marinas and Leyte convinced the 32nd Army staff that the attack would come in late March or early April.

From an early date the principle guiding the Japanese plan of defence was that, since it was impossible to defeat the invading enemy, the most successful plan would be that which denied him the use of the island for as long a period as possible and caused him the greatest casualties. The following plans were suggested, the first being that which was adopted.

1. To defend, from extensive underground positions, the Shimajiri sector (i.e. that part of Okinawa south of the Naha–Shuri–Yonabaru line) the main line of defences being north of Naha, Shuri, and Yonabaru. Landings north of this line were not be opposed; landings south of the line would be met on the beaches. Since it would be impossible to defend Kadena airfield 15cm guns were to be emplaced so as to bring fire against the airfield and deny the invaders its use.

2. To defend from prepared positions the central portion of the island, including the Kadena and Yontan airfields.

3. To dispose one division around the Kadena area, one division in the southern end of the island, and one brigade between the two divisions. To meet the enemy wherever he landed and attempt to annihilate him on the beaches.

4. To defend the northern part of the island with Army Headquarters in Nago and the main line of defence based on Hill 830 north-east of Yontan airfield The proponents of this course maintained that the terrain in northern Okinawa was most favourable for prolonging the defence although, admittedly, the loss of the more highly developed southern section was undesirable.

Although the withdrawal of the 9th Division seriously weakened the forces available for the defence of Okinawa the move was not opposed by 32nd Army since the division was removed with the intention of using it to reinforce the Philippines. Pleas for reinforcements from Japan were made in vain to Tokyo. There was a faint hope of getting reinforcements before L-Day, but, Colonel Yahara states, none whatsoever thereafter.

The plan which was adopted, i.e. to defend the Shuri line, pre-supposed US occupation of Kadena and Yontan airfields. Although there was some pressure from Tokyo and certain individuals within 32nd Army to include Kadena airfield within the zone of defence this was deemed impractical, since, due to considerations of terrain, the defence of Kadena would seriously over-extend forces barely sufficient for the effective defence of the southern part of the island.

The building of airfields on Ie Jima was criticised, since it was impossible to defend the island for more than a few days. Accordingly, on 10 March demolition of the airfields was initiated. Subsequently, 4 x 15cm guns were emplaced in positions on the Motobu peninsula from where they could be brought to bear on Ie.

The beaches originally considered most probable for US landings were:

(a) the Hagushi beaches,

(b) the Gusukuma beaches (i.e. the beaches west of Machinato airfield)

(c) the coast between Naha and Itoman

(d) the Minatoga beaches and

(e) the Nakagusuku Wan beaches.

By the end of March it was expected that the main US strength, probably 6–10 divisions would land upon the Hagushi beaches, immediately securing the Kadena and Yontan airfields.

It was believed that the invading forces might, following the initial landings, establish beachhead perimeters each two divisions in strength, 1½ to 3 kilometres in depth, each division holding 3km of beach. The perimeters would be maintained until enough supplies had been landed to permit a large-scale attack, using massed tanks and concentrated artillery fire. The invaders would rely upon material strength to wear down the defenders rather than making a frontal assault It was estimated that about ten days would be required to get the Hagushi forces in position to attack the main defence line based on Shuri and that during that time the US hoped to force the Japanese to move their main force to the Shuri line and then to effect a not too costly landing, probably by one division, on the coast somewhere south of Shuri probably Minatogawa. Additional landings on Ie Jima were expected but the landings on Kerama came as a surprise, foiling their plans for conducting suicide boat warfare.

Artillery was ordered not to fire upon US shipping and divisions were instructed not to oppose US reconnaissance or initial landings in their sectors until sufficient troops had been brought ashore to render it difficult to effect an escape by boat. The purpose was two fold:

(a) to attempt to deceive US intelligence as to the disposition of the Japanese forces;

(b) to ensure that any attack on US beachhead positions would engage and 'annihilate' a sizeable force.

The weakest point of the final defence plan was considered to be the Chinen Peninsula. Landings on Chinen would give the invaders good observation to direct naval gunfire and a position from which to launch an attack upon the heart of the defensive line.

Accordingly only the 62nd Division, considered to be their best and most experienced outfit, was moved into the Shuri line, leaving the main force prepared to annihilate any enemy force unwise enough to attempt landing to the south. The 5th Artillery Command was ordered to place all its component elements in defence of the Minatogawa sector. The Artillery Command CP was established near Itokazu (TS 8364 R2 [a map reference]). The initial US diversion on the east coast increased their hopes that a landing would be attempted and contributed to the great reluctance with which troops were drawn from the south to strengthen the Shuri line.

Until the end of April enough troops were left in the south to deal a severe blow to any landing. Hope of defending the southern coast was given up following the abortive counter-attack of 4th May. A new plan was devised by which, in the event of a landing, 2–3,000 troops would fight a delaying action while the main force, giving up Naha and Yonabaru, would establish a circular perimeter around Shuri extending as far south as Tuskazan.

The absence of a landing puzzled the 32nd Army staff, particularly after the beginning of May when it became impossible to put up more than a token resistance in the south. Prevailing opinion was that the Tenth Army wished to obtain as cheap a victory as possible by wearing down the Shuri line rather than committing elements to a possibly hazardous landing in the south in the interests of bringing the operation to a speedier end.

Plans for fleet support of ground forces in the defence of Okinawa were contemplated but never emerged from a rather nebulous stage. Coordination of such activities was in the hands of the Okinawa Base Force. 32nd Army also maintained direct liaison with the Navy General Staff which actually showed more interest in the campaign than did the Army General Staff. No naval personnel ashore were specifically charged with direction of naval gunfire should fleet units succeed in reaching Okinawa.

The 32nd Army profited from the lesson learned on Saipan where Japanese artillery had been wiped out in the first days of the operation. The overall command of artillery on Okinawa was in the hands of the 5th Artillery Command.

The factors responsible for the failure of Japanese artillery in the past were thought to be:

(1) The lack of cave positions, preferably such that the piece could be fired from inside the cave; and

(2) Premature firing, exposing positions before real damage could be done the enemy.

Consequently, under the Artillery Command's direction, preparations were made for concealing the guns, emplaced in the elaborate system of caves encountered later by US forces. Extensive surveying was conducted by the Artillery Survey Company, supplying all artillery units with data and expediting the problem of transfer and massing of fire.

The Japanese realised that ammunition was insufficient for a protracted campaign. Impassioned pleas to Tokyo brought only the information that the shipping situation was acute. The Japanese prepared, accordingly, to make the most efficient use of available ammunition.

The calibre of the Japanese general officers charged with the defence of Okinawa was uniformly high. The following comments by Colonel Yahara throw some light on the characters of the defeated commanders.

Lt-General Ushijima, Mitsuru, General Officer Commanding-in-Chief 32nd Army. A quiet, reserved but extremely capable officer, held in the highest esteem by all men of his command. He was regarded by some as a latter-day Saigo Takamori (a military hero of the time of the Meiji Restoration). He delegated all authority to his subordinates, yet took the full responsibility for any decisions made by them. Although an able

tactician he took little part in the actual planning; his position was, in fact, little more than an eminently suitable figurehead.

Lt-General Cho, Isamu, Chief of Staff; 32nd Army. A fiery individual possessed of tremendous energy, Cho was the driving force behind the 32nd Army. Quick to anger and demanding, Cho was not universally popular, but no one questioned his ability. Cho made no bones about his epicurean tastes; his cellar was well stocked with better brands of sake and an ample supply of Scotch whisky. Colonel Yahara believes that Ushijima and Cho made a perfect combination, Ushijima acting as the balance wheel on Cho's drive.

Lt-General Fujioka, Takeo, General Officer Commanding 62nd Division. Not a War College graduate, Fujioka came up through field commands. Quiet and conservative, he was considered the embodiment of the samurai type. Like Ushijima he relied heavily on his chief of staff.

Lt-General Amamya, Tatsumi, General Officer Commanding 24th Division. In temperament Amamya resembled Fujioka, although more inclined to exert his personal authority. Hardworking and competent, he was regarded as an excellent leader.

Maj-General Suzuki, Shigeji, General Officer Commanding, 44th IMB. The least respected of the generals, Suzuki expressed some resentment that Fujioka, who graduated below him at the JMA, should hold higher rank. He did a competent job, though handicapped by a lack of experienced staff officers.

c. Enemy Operations

The tactical direction of the defence resolved itself into a struggle between the conservatives, including Colonel Yahara who advocated strictly defensive warfare, and a group of radicals who proposed that the Japanese take the offensive whenever there seemed to be the slightest possibility of succeeding.

An ill conceived plan for a counter-attack on 8th April was proposed at a staff meeting on 5th or 6th April. At that time the 62nd Division alone was on the line, eager to take offensive action. It was proposed to bring up the 24th Division, 44th IMB, and all major artillery units and in one massed blow to drive the invaders to the Ishikawa isthmus. The 62nd Division was to spearhead the attack, having as its objective Hill 220 northeast of Yontan airfield. The 24th Division was to follow, then veer to the east, driving up the east coast. The 44th IMB was to be held in reserve.

Left: Marines pass through a small village on Okinawa past Japanese dead.

The plan met with the vigorous opposition of Colonel Yahara and other cooler heads among the staff officers who reasoned that even if the attack should succeed initially the Japanese would be at the mercy of US naval gunfire and bombing since no positions had been prepared in the area. Also, the south would be left defenceless against possible landings. The plan was accordingly dropped, reluctantly by a group of fire-eaters, the majority deciding that only a madman could envision the success of such a venture. Another factor influencing the decision was a belief that the US forces might set up a defensive line south of the Awase peninsula, and proceed with the securing of the northern part of the island, putting off the reduction of the south indefinitely.

The proponents of aggressive action finally were permitted to attempt a counter-attack on the night of 12th April. The failure of the venture strengthened Yahara's position as the spokesman of the conservatives.

The 62nd Division was still holding the line alone with the 22nd Regiment of the 24th Division in reserve in the Nishibaru area. On the night of 9th or 10th April plans were drawn up at a staff meeting calling for three battalions of the 22nd Regiment and three battalions of the 62nd Division to infiltrate, scattering throughout the area between the lines and the objective line,

1,500 yards north of Futema The sector lines ran through the centre of the island, with the 62nd Division on the west and the 22nd Regiment on the east. Within each sector one battalion was to occupy the northern one-third of the area, another battalion the centre one-third, and the last battalion the southern third. The men were to hide in caves and tombs, awaiting a suitable opportunity to attack on 13th April.

The main advantage of the attack was that it would prevent the use of US naval gunfire or artillery since the area would be occupied simultaneously by US and Japanese troops, thus enabling the Japanese to fight upon their own terms, i.e. hand-to-hand combat. On the other hand, the 22nd Regiment was unfamiliar with the terrain. As it turned out, this factor accounted for the complete failure of the attack.

Colonel Yahara opposed the attack and succeeded in reducing the forces participating to four battalions.

The attack was launched as scheduled. As Colonel Yahara had predicted, the battalions of the 22nd Regiment were bewildered by the terrain and by dawn had made only 500 yards. They were forced to retire at, suffering heavy casualties. The 62nd Division battalions fared somewhat better, one battalion advancing to TA 83782, remaining there throughout the day of 13th April and returning that night with low casualties.

On about 20th April, after the loss of Tanabaru, the Japanese began to move troops north in anticipation of a US landing in the Yonabaru area. The 62nd Division, reinforced on the right (east) flank by the 22nd Regiment was holding a line from Onaga–Hill 187 to the Machinato airfield. Even the blindest staff officer was growing aware that US forces would eventually break through any defences the Japanese could establish. As yet the Japanese had not suffered crippling casualties and in the opinion of many officers the time was ripe to strike a 'decisive' blow.

General Cho, always a proponent of aggressive action, was instrumental in the decision to stage the counter-attack. Cho was vigorously supported by Fujioka, commander of the 62nd Division, who expressed the general desire of his men to fight the decisive action in the 62nd Division's zone of defence. Colonel Yahara opposed the attack as being premature but was over-ridden.

The plan was ambitious. The 23rd and 26th Shipping Engineer Regiments were to effect counter-landings on the east and west coast respectively during the night of 3rd–4th May. On 4th May the 24th Division (89th Regiment on the east, 22nd Regiment in the centre, and 32nd Regiment on the west) were to launch an attack with Futema as the objective. The 44th IMB was to follow the 24th Division, bearing west to the coast, thus cutting off the 1st Marine Division. The 62nd Division did not participate in the attack.

It was, it is Colonel Yahara's opinion, the decisive action of the campaign. The Japanese were so weakened by its failure that they lost all hope of taking any further offensive action.

On 5th May General Ushijima called Colonel Yahara to his office and, with tears in his eyes, declared that he would, in the future, be guided by Yahara's decisions.

On about 20th May it became apparent to the 32nd Army staff that the line north of Shuri would be soon untenable. The pressure exerted upon the line from both Sugar Loaf and Conical Hills forced a decision as to whether or not to stage the last ditch stand at Shuri. The capture of Sugar Loaf Hill alone could have been solved by the withdrawal of the left flank to positions south of Naha and, in Colonel Yahara's opinion would not have seriously endangered the defence of Shuri. However, the loss of remaining positions on Conical Hill in conjunction with the pressure in the west rendered the defence of Shuri extremely difficult.

Below: US ships setting up an AAA and rocket barrage against Japanese kamikazes.

On the night of 21st May a conference attended by all division and brigade commanders was held in the 32nd Army headquarters caves under Shuri Castle. Three possible courses of action were proposed:

(1) Make the final stand at Shuri;

(2) Withdraw to the Chinen Peninsula;

(3) Withdraw to the south.

The first plan was favoured by the 62nd Division which was reluctant to withdraw from what it thought of as its own territory. Other factors favouring the adoption of this plan were the presence of large quantities of stores in Shuri and a general feeling that a withdrawal would not be in the best traditions of the Japanese Army. It was recognised that to stay would result in a quicker defeat and consequently this option was discarded in accord with the 32nd Army policy of protracting the struggle as long as possible. A retreat to Chinen was regarded with no great favour by anyone and was deemed unfeasible due to the difficulties of transportation over rough and mountainous terrain. The discussion resolved in a decision to conduct an ordered retreat to the south, influenced to a great extent by the presence of 24th Division positions and stores in that area.

The transport of supplies and wounded began on the night of 22nd May. The burden of the operation was in the hands of the 24th Transport Regiment, an unusually proficient organisation commanded by a Colonel Nakamur who later received a commendation for the masterful way in which the operation was carried out. While in China the Regiment had been intensively trained in night driving, apparently with some success.

The occupation of Yonabaru on 23rd May came as a surprise to the Japanese who did not expect such a move during the inclement weather prevailing at that time, assuming that US infantry would be unwilling to attack without tanks which were thought to be immobilised by the mud. On 23rd May elements of the 24th Division were despatched to retake the town. The attack continued with no success on the 24th and 25th May.

At this time the 62nd Division sector consisted only of less than a 2,000 yard front north of Shuri held by one battalion. The main force, consisting of about 3,000 men was in Shuri, several hundred yards to the rear. Since the pressure directly north of Shuri was relatively light it was decided to place the battalion on the line under the command of the 24th Division and to send the rest of the 62nd Division to assist the 24th Division in the attack on Yonabaru. On 25th May the 62nd Division left Shuri and, travelling by a circuitous route, approached Yonabaru from the south, three days being required for the manoeuvre. The arrival of the 62nd Division failed to relieve the situation.

Above: *Admiral William F. Halsey, Commander, 3rd Fleet.*

The mass retreat from Shuri took place during the night of 29th May. Combat units left between 50% and 30% of their troops behind to hold the line for another day with orders to retreat on the night of the 30th. A temporary line from the mouth of the Kokuba Gawa on the west coast running north of Tsukazn to TA 8089 and then bearing south through Karadera to Hill 157 in TA 8367 was occupied on 1st–2nd June with the 44th IMB manning the sector from the west coast to Kokuba, the 24th Division from Kokuba to Chan, and the 62nd Division from Chan to the east coast.

The 44th IMB retreated through Itoman then bore east going north of Makabe and through Medeera to occupy the western portion of the line based on Yaeju Dake, arriving on 3rd June. The remnants of the 62nd Division (2,500 men) fell back through Tamamkabe and Gusuku Mura and Gushichan Mura occupying the sector south of Makabe and west of Mabuni Dake on 4th June. The 24th Division (7–8,000 men) withdrew through the centre of the island, taking up the east flank on 4th June.

The message from General Buckner offering Ushijima an opportunity to surrender did not arrive at 32nd Army Headquarters until 17th June, a week after it had been dropped behind the Japanese lines. Colonel Yahara states that the delay was normal for front line to headquarters communications at that stage of the operation. The message was delivered to Colonel Yahara who passed it to General Cho, after showing it to his staff officers. The staff officers were unimpressed and treated the matter lightly. General Ushijima's reaction is not recorded.

d. Enemy Intelligence

32nd Army intelligence was admittedly poor. Although a staff officer was charged with intelligence he was hampered by assignment to other duties and by the general lack of interest in intelligence among front-line troops. Division staff officers looked upon intelligence as minor matter; below division, there were no personnel concerned with intelligence. Colonel Yahara admits that an unfortunate attitude that intelligence work belonged properly only to officers incompetent for operations work prevailed even in the highest echelon.

Colonel Yahara states that the greatest single source of intelligence was US news broadcasts identifying units on the island and describing the general progress of the operation. Such broadcasts were monitored in Taiwan and transmitted from there to Okinawa.

Practically the only other sources of intelligence were documents taken from bodies and wrecked tanks. Although a civil service official supposedly qualified in the English language was assigned to Army headquarters, he proved himself incompetent and Colonel Yahara read captured documents personally. A tank destroyed shortly after the 27th Division came into the line yielded an operation plan of that division. The document was taken to 32nd Army Headquarters where it was examined by Colonel Yahara. Most of the document was not of immediate interest, however, the 'Estimate of Enemy Capabilities' aroused great interest and amusement. On 5th May a Marine enemy situation map, captured during the 4th May counter-attack caused great consternation because of its accurate appraisal of Japanese dispositions. Some valuable order of battle information was taken from addresses on personal letters taken from US dead. The presence of the 1st Marine Division on the southern line was discovered in this fashion.

The only US POWs of which Colonel Yahara admits knowledge are one navy ensign or lt (jg) shot down off Kerama and two or three unidentified flyers captured in March. The first POW was interrogated on Okinawa and apparently revealed movements of his task force (it is not known how accurately; the Japanese accepted his account at face value) but when questioned as to future operations advised his interrogators to consult Admiral Nimitz. This POW was subsequently flown to Tokyo for more intensive interrogation. Colonel Yahara can furnish no information on the POWs captured in March, beyond the fact that he thinks they were flown to Tokyo immediately to be worked over by competent interrogators. No

Above: Chester W. Nimitz, Commander in Chief, US Pacific Fleet, showing the new insignia of Fleet Admiral, the rank to which he was elevated on 19th December 1944.

POWs were reported to 32nd Army Headquarters during the operation; if any were taken they were dealt with on the spot. Orders directing units to attempt to take prisoners were issued with no results. Several Okinawans suspected of acting as US agents were turned in but, without exception, they were found to be insane.

Occasionally staff officers listened in on US voice transmission but, due to their imperfect English, gained no information of any value.

Indicative of the character of Japanese intelligence are two reports received at Army headquarters. The first, received shortly after the 1st Marine Division moved into the southern line stated that Chinese and Negro marines had been observed being driven to the front by tanks, presumably to prevent their desertion. A second report, received from an infiltration team, described a gala party, complete with orchestra, Chinese lanterns and dancing girls, which had purportedly been seen in progress at Futema

e. Battle Lessons

The 32nd Army staff was somewhat puzzled by certain phases of US tactics which were in conflict with accepted Japanese tactical doctrines.

The US attack against the Japanese line was often characterised by the exertion of uniform pressure against the

entire line. When weak points were discovered in the Japanese line they were generally probed by US patrols yet no efforts were made to effect a break-through, if only to gain a temporary advantage. This seemed at variance with what the Japanese considered sound tactics, which would advise an attack in force upon weak points with the objective of causing the enemy heavy casualties, if not of disrupting his defence. The seemingly over cautious policy came as a disappointment to many Japanese staff officers who had hoped to force a decision once the US forces had engaged the Shuri defence line and before the Japanese had been appreciably reduced in strength.

Colonel Yahara and other staff officers became of the opinion that the Tenth Army had been committed to taking the island as cheaply as possible. In retrospect he declares that the policy was probably wise, insofar as it reduced total casualties, although more aggressive action would probably have shortened the campaign appreciably.

US methods of tank warfare also came as a surprise to the Japanese. Colonel Yahara expressed the belief of the Japanese that Okinawa was ideally suited to large scale tank warfare, at least in comparison with the home islands of Japan. (In this connection, Colonel Yahara remarked that the Chiba Peninsula was probably the only area in Japan suited by terrain for armoured warfare. The Japanese themselves find difficulty in conducting manoeuvres on terrain characterised by paddy fields and irrigation systems.) The Japanese envisioned US tank attacks comparable in scale to those of the European war, involving five or six waves of 100 tanks each. Indications that such attacks were not contemplated came as a great relief to the Japanese. Colonel Yahara is, however, of the opinion that US superiority in tanks was the single factor most important in deciding the battle of Okinawa.

The Japanese were forced to admit that their counter-measures were ineffective. Anti-tank guns were of little use in well concealed positions and were soon destroyed if moved to positions with better fields of fire; suicide attacks by personnel bearing explosive charges were disappointing; bringing artillery fire against tanks was difficult because of poor communication and the undesirability of firing during the daytime when under air observation. Some comfort was derived from the observation that tanks would sometimes withdraw in the face of a show of strength or when accompanying infantry were fired upon.

At one point there was a rather wistful discussion of the possibility of retrieving damaged US tanks and after repairing them to use them in the field. The scheme soon proved to be impractical. A light anti-tank weapon such as the bazooka is badly needed by the Japanese.

The tactical manoeuvre causing the greatest concern to the Japanese was the so called horseback attack (umanori kogeki), i.e. the double envelopment of cave positions. Although the Japanese positions were constructed so as to be mutually self-supporting certain unexpected factors entered the picture. It was discovered that double-envelopment tactics had been successful not so much because of inherent defects in the construction of the position but simply because troops in nearby positions were reluctant to endanger their own safety by opening fire on positions which had been enveloped. Orders were issued that an officer or NCO would remain on watch at all times in each position and that there would be no delay in opening fire upon US troops attacking other positions.

flamethrowers were countered by constructing caves with the main passages at right angles to the entrance. To minimise further the effect of flamethrowers, entrances are covered with blankets, shelter-halves or other heavy materials thoroughly wetted. Colonel Yahara believes that these measures were fairly successful against brief attacks, although admittedly unable to withstand prolonged attack.

US night attacks were particularly effective, taking the Japanese completely by surprise. The Japanese had so

Above: Prisoner of war camp near Kamiyama town in hills of Honshu, Japan. Planes from the USS Bennington *(CV-20) discovered this camp and the next day dropped food packages. The prisoner's expression of gratitude can be seen – TNX – a telegraphic form of 'Thanks' in the yard of the camp.*

Left: More than 50 US Navy carrier-based SB2C Helldivers, TBM Avengers and F6F Hellcats flying past Mount Fujyama on their way to bomb the Japanese capital of Tokyo.

accustomed themselves to ceasing organised hostilities at nightfall and, except for the ubiquitous Kirikomitai, reorganising and relaxing during the night, that attacks in these hours caught them both physically and psychologically off guard. Colonel Yahara believes that such attacks could have been successfully exploited to a much greater extent than they were.

The 32nd Army had experienced considerable bombing and was reasonably certain that its cave positions gave adequate protection. There was, however, general consternation at the prospect of being under naval gunfire. Colonel Yahara was informed by an artillery officer that battleships had firepower equivalent to the artillery of seven infantry divisions; this naturally caused him some anxiety which was relieved only

Above: Incendiary bombs fill the air over Yokohama on 29th May 1945. Almost seven square miles of Yokohama were devastated in this daylight raid by almost 500 B-29s of the US 21st Bomber Command.

when, after the first naval bombardment of the island, he inspected the results and found that well constructed cave positions were vulnerable only to direct hits. The following conclusions were drawn as to the effectiveness against naval gunfire, bombing, and artillery fire:

1. Naval gunfire, bombing, and artillery directed against an area the size of Okinawa will not have much effect against disciplined troops in well-constructed cave positions. Important positions must be such that no amount of bombing or shelling will destroy them.

2. After positions have been overrun or destroyed by the enemy dispersion is vital. All movements must be at night.

3. The final result will be by hand-to-hand combat.

The enemy's first taste of US artillery was the bombardment by pieces emplaced on Keise Shima, which caused the enemy no little annoyance, particularly since they had not anticipated any such move. Counter-battery brought against those batteries was believed to be partially successful.

The effectiveness of US artillery was countered, successfully to a great extent, by the elaborate system of underground fortifications. Heavy bombardments such as came before attacks caused relatively low casualties.

US observation planes were a constant threat to the Japanese. They learned quickly that the presence of an observation plane overhead usually presaged enemy fire, and, although they appeared to present fine targets, observation planes were tantalisingly hard to hit with small arms. Observation planes were, therefore, treated with great respect, all movement being kept to an absolute minimum while these planes were overhead.

MR SHIMADA
Secretary to Lt-General Cho – chief of staff 32nd Army Age: 35, Captured: at Guhichan

ASSESSMENT
1. Details of Capture
POW claims to have been the last member of the of 32nd Army staff to leave the Army CP on Hill 89 at Mabuni (TS 7857) on 24th June. With no particular purpose in mind, he attempted to make his way northward, but was captured by 7th Division Military Police later the same day at Guschichan. At the time of capture he was carrying on his person the only remaining copies of personal letters written by General Cho, before his death, to the Minister of War, the head of the Imperial Rule Assistance

Above: The aftermath of the bombing of Yokahoma, as seen after the surrender of Japan. Some 85% of the city is said to have been destroyed.

Association, the Poetry Master of the Imperial Household and other officials. These were taken away from POW and thrown aside by the Military Police who searched him. Returning to the spot two days later in the company of intelligence personnel he found only a few burned fragments of the documents.

2. Evaluation

POW is an extremely shrewd individual blessed with a glib tongue and a very rational way of thinking. His memory and powers of observation are excellent and the reliability of his information is far above that of the average officer POW. Impelled by motives of expediency as well as idealism, he has offered his services to the United States to assist the speedy winning of the war in whatever way he can. From his background, general knowledge and native ability, it seems evident that he could be of great service in this connection; he has already given information which should lead to the apprehension of at least one important 32nd Army staff officer.

For the past eight years POW was an intimate friend of the late Lt-General Cho Isamu, chief of staff, 32nd Army and he served as Cho's personal secretary throughout the campaign. (His official rank in this capacity was that of a Higher Civil Service Official of the Sixth Class – equivalent to a captain in the military.) His association with General Cho and other members of the 32nd Army staff has enabled him to contribute considerable information not previously known about the plans and activities of the 32nd Army during the battle for Okinawa. In addition his former affiliation with the *Tokumu Kikan* the Japanese secret intelligence organisation, should be of great interest and POW's knowledge of this agency, as well the large body of general information in his possession should be further exploited by detailed higher echelon interrogation.

3. Intelligence

Chronology

1932   Entered Army – 13th Infantry Regiment.
1933   Commissioned 2nd Lieutenant, released from service.
1933–39 In civilian occupations.
1939   Joined *Tokumu Kikan* (see details later in report). Transferred to Peking.
1941   Discharged from *Tokumu Kikan*.
1945   Served as Lt-General Cho's private secretary.

32nd Army Operations

The 32nd Army was activated on 1st April 1944 and put under the command of Lt-General Watanabe Masao, with Maj-General Kitagawa Masao as chief of staff; the original headquarters were at Asato (TS 7572) northeast of Naha. In the summer and early autumn of that year the units which were to form the main strength of the 32nd Army arrived in Okinawa and plans were made for hastening defence preparations on the island.

General Watanabe had been in poor health since arriving on Okinawa and consequently was unable to play any active part in the direction of his command. As the chief of staff was considered a rather ineffective personality and a second-rate strategist, the Watanabe–Kitagawa combination left much to be desired and it was replaced at the end of August 1944 by Lt-General Ushijima Mitsuru as the commanding general and Lt-General Cho Isamu as chief of staff. (Lt-General Watanabe is no longer on active service; Kitagawa is assistant chief of staff 10th Area Army.) Ushijima arrived immediately before the departure of his predecessor; Cho, however, remained in Tokyo for final staff conferences at IGHQ and did not reach Okinawa until late in September. (It should be noted that prior to assuming his post as chief of staff, Cho had visited Okinawa in June or July 1944 as a tactical adviser from IGHQ and had held conferences with the 32nd Army staff at that time.)

After the arrival of Ushijima and Cho there were considerable revisions made in the personnel at 32nd Army staff section. The staff which emerged was in general distinguished by its ability, comparative youth and low rank – there was an unusually large number of majors in positions which might ordinarily be occupied by officers of the higher field grades. Even General Cho and Colonel Yahara, the senior staff officer, were young for their rank and responsibility.

With the reorganisation of the 32nd Army staff completed, work was hurried on the defence plans of the island. The withdrawal of the 9th Division to Formosa in December on the orders of IGHQ made the situation critical, as it became evident that Japan lacked sufficient shipping to send any reinforcements to Okinawa to replace this unit. In January General Cho went to Tokyo for a final conference at IGHQ on the strategy to be used in the defence of Okinawa. It was at this conference that Cho was told that 32nd Army units were not to fire on US shipping in the event of an attempted landing on Okinawa; IGHQ assured him that the kamikaze suicide planes and similar units were enough to ensure the destruction of the greater part of US naval forces without forcing shore batteries to give away their positions by premature firing.

After the departure of Watanabe, Army headquarters was moved to Shuri and in January 1945 work was begun enlarging the system of caves beneath Shuri Castle for eventual use as 32nd Army CP. Construction continued on field fortifications for the various Army units and in February POW accompanied the chief of staff on an extended inspection of the positions to the north of Shuri, at which time Cho criticised and changed various entrenchments along the lines.

Commencing in January 1945 an effort was made to mobilise virtually the entire civilian manpower of Okinawa for use as Army auxiliaries. Additional Home Guard levies were made, designed to supplement the earlier conscriptions of the autumn of 1944. Almost the entire student body of the Middle Schools, the Vocational Schools and the Shuri Normal School was organised into guerrilla units, the most prominent of which was the celebrated Blood-and-Iron-for-the-Emperor Duty Unit [Tekketsu Kinno Tai]. The students were trained in infiltration tactics by a Captain Hirose, an expert on guerrilla warfare who had been sent to 32nd Army from IGHQ for the express purpose of coordinating the activities of infiltration groups and similar irregular forces.

On 10 February 1945, POW was told by General Cho that word had been received from IGHQ that no invasion of Okinawa was imminent. On 15 February the last passenger ship for Japan left Okinawa with a cargo composed mainly of refugees. From that time (with the exception of several small ships the last of which left Okinawa in early March) there was no surface communication between Okinawa and the Japanese home islands. Continuous radio communication was of course maintained until the very end of the campaign with Tokyo, Formosa and the other islands of the Ryukyus. However, from the time of US landings IGHQ made no attempt to interfere in the conduct of the Okinawa campaign nor did the Formosan Army (10th Area Army); 32nd Army directed its own operation from start to finish.

When in late March it became evident that the US landing was about to take place, the 32nd Army staff was faced with the problem of a final disposition of its forces to deal with the invasion in the most effective way possible. It was already committed to a defence of Shimajiri Gun and accordingly had evacuated its main strength from most of Okinawa to the southern part of the island, leaving behind the so-called Kunigami Detachment to defend the north as long as possible. (Although this course meant the virtual abandonment of the Yontan and Kadena airfields to US forces, it was felt that the advantages of fighting with forces concentrated in a restricted area easily defended both by location and the nature of the terrain more than compensated for the loss.) In addition a landing on the Hagushi beaches or possibly further south on the west coast was expected. The pressing question was whether or not an additional landing – possibly the principal one – would be made on the eastern coast off Minatogawa (where a US landing feint was later made). There was a long and sharp discussion on this point among the staff members. Colonel Yahara, the senior staff officer, insisted that a diversionary landing would at some time be made in the Minatogawa region; in order to crush this move it was necessary to keep a sizeable portion of the Army's strength in that area, i.e. south of the Shuri–Yonabaru line. Major Yakumaru, the Intelligence officer, held that no such landing would be made and that the only US landing would come in force on the Hagushi beaches or thereabouts. Needless to say, Yahara's prestige and arguments won the day and POW records that Yakumaru, bitterly disappointed at the final decision, went off for the next few days to inundate his sorrows in prolonged draughts of expensive sake.

As a result of the staff's decision, the L-Day dispositions of the principal 32nd Army units were as follows:

The 62nd Division with Headquarters at Shuri Castle had its component units disposed north of the Shuri area in northern Shimajiri and southern Nakagami Gun;

The 12th II [Independent Infantry] Bn was farthest north with a front line running through Oyama, Futim (TS 8481), Ataniya (TS 8681) and Kuba (TS 8980);

The 63rd Brigade had its CP at Nakama (TS 7975), with the 13th II Bn along the Kakazu line (TS 7668);

The 14th II Bn on a line from Nishibaru to Kaniku;

The 11th II Bn on the Tanabaru (TS 8275);

Ouki front; the 64th Brigade with Headquarters at Dakeshi (TS 7874) held the coast sector from Machinato (TS 7978) to Amiku (TS 7473).

The 24th Division with Headquarters at Yoza (TS 7661) was deployed south of Shuri in central and southern Shimajiri Gun. Its sector was bounded on the west by Matambashi (TS 7669), Tomigusuku (TS 7468), Gibo, Takamine, (TS 7360) and Aragon; on the east by Gushichan, Minatogawa (TS 8361), Aragusuku (TS 8162), Kamizato (TS 8066), Toyama (TS 8462), Furugen (TS 8190), and Kanegusuku (TS 7367).

The 44th IMB occupied the Chinen (TS 9165) Peninsula area with its sector bounded on the west by Minatogawa, Takamiyagusuku (TS 7268) and Itarashiku (TS 8469), the brigade CP was at Takamiyagusuku.

The Okinawa Naval Base Force was charged with the defence of the Oroku Peninsula.

In addition to the above major echelons with their attached units there was a considerable body of provisional infantry troops available as a reserve. In accordance with previously laid plans, the greater part of 32nd Army service and specialised troops had been converted to an infantry organisation at the time of US landing. In general they were held in rear areas until later in the campaign.

The first and for a short time the only unit to engage US troops was the 12th II Bn; by 4th/5th April short shrift had been made of this detachment and the remnants drew back along the coast coast in an attempt to reach 62nd Division Headquarters at Shuri. As the lines pushed southward it soon became for the Japanese a question of holding to the line from Kakazu through Nishibaru to Tanabaru in the 63rd Brigade sector. By the latter part of April the 62nd Division had sustained heavy losses and Army decided that it was necessary to strengthen the division's front. Accordingly, one battalion of Army infantry [IN: under the direct control of 32nd Army], one regiment of the 24th Division [IN: 22nd Regiment] and another element of the 44th IMB were sent to the line in front of Futema on about 20th April as reinforcements; they were attached to the 62nd Division.

At the beginning of May plans were made for a counter-attack on the eastern side of the front, using all three infantry regiments of the 24th Division. On the night of 3rd May there was a conference of brigade and division commanding generals at the Shuri headquarters and final arrangements for the attack were made. The order to the units involved was given that night and the attack began on the morning of the next day. It had for its objective penetration of US lines on a wide front as far as Futema which was believed to be the Tenth Army CP area. Despite the ambitious aim of this assault, it met with no success; on the contrary the Japanese were forced to fall back to a line extending from Yafuso (TS 7775) through Nakama, Maeda (TS 8075), Kochi (TS 8174), and Gaja (TS 8372). It was after this ill-starred action (the failure of which was attributed partly to transport difficulties in bringing the troops up to the line) that General Cho abandoned all hope of a successful outcome of the operation and declared that only time intervened between defeat and the 32nd Army.

To bolster the lines, a battalion of Shipping Engineers [IN: probably the remainder of the 26th Shipping Engineer Regiment] under Lt-Colonel Haraga was moved into the line from Amiku (TS 7573) along the Asagawa and the main strength of the 44th IMB took up positions on the Asato–Amiku line; by this time the 24th Division had taken over the old 62nd Division sector; the 62nd Division, which had been very roughly handled in the past month, occupied the zone between the 24th and the 44th IMB. In the Tsyukazan (TS 7868)–Naha area to the south, the 32nd Army Freight Depot, the Ordnance Depot and other service units had been organised into two provisional infantry battalions with headquarters at Kakazu. These were to cooperate with the Ozato Guard Unit [IN: An informally named provisional infantry unit with attached Navy units which was posted at the approaches to the Chinen Peninsula] in opposing a possible US breakthrough or landing behind the lines.

It is interesting to note that throughout this time and until the evacuation of Shuri the 32nd Army was constantly expecting an attack by US paratroops. Patrols were continually posted – particularly in the Tsukazan sector, where it was thought an attack would be most likely – to guard against this eventuality.

By the latter part of May the situation of the Shuri line had become increasingly critical and US successes on both flanks of the line threatened ultimately to isolate the defenders in the city and the surrounding areas. Accordingly a staff meeting of the 32nd Army unit commanders was held at the Army CP to decide on the next move. One group led by Lt-General Fujioka, commander of 62nd Division, advocated remaining in Shuri for a last stand. Although this view seemed for a time to prevail, it was ultimately decided to withdraw to the Mabuni area and orders were given to all units to make their retreat at the end of the month. On 22nd May 32nd Army Headquarters moved from 21:00 until dawn, organised into four echelons, the Commanding General of the 32nd Army was in the second echelon which moved to Tsukazan by way of Shichina and Ichinichibashi (TS 7869). The third echelon, which included the chief of staff, made its way to Tsukazan via Hantagawa and the south Haebaru road. After the departure of the fourth echelon, demolition squads under a Captain Hayakawa were left behind in various points of the Army CP to carry out demolition work.

32nd Army Headquarters staff personnel spent two nights in Tsukazan and proceeded to Mabuni in two 24th Division trucks, followed by the Headquarters troops, From 1st June to the end operations were directed from the Army C.P at Hill 89–Mabuni. (As an indication of the nature of 32nd Army staff's withdrawal, it should be noted that only 20 days' supply of rations were taken from the Army C.P.)

The remnants of 32nd Army retreated from Shuri, fighting as they went and attempted to regroup for a last stand in the

Right: The explosion of the first atomic bomb dropped from Enola Gay on Hiroshima 6th August 1945.

southern part of Sehjajiri Gun. The 24th Division established its CP at Madeera (TS 7759) with its units disposed on a line extending through Nakagusuku (TS 7258) Kuniyoshi, Osato (TS 7561), Yaezu Dake (TS 7861), and Oka. The last of the 62nd Division and other 32nd Army units held a final resistance line on Hill 96.3 north of Mabuni and Komesu (TS 7657). 44th IMB concentrated at Gushichan and Nakaza.

As a result of continual US pressure, the remaining Japanese troops by 20th June had been pushed into two pockets – one in the Mabuni, Komesu and Yamagusuku area with the Hill 89 CP as its centre and the other, composed mainly of 24th Division troops, isolated at Madeera. On 19th June a final meeting of the Army staff was held, at which General Cho ordered certain staff members to leave the island for the purpose of conveying various official messages and comments on the operation to IGHQ. These officers were to make their way north – in civilian clothes – from Mabuni to Okuko (TS 4048) at the northwestern end of the island; from there they were to proceed to Tokuno Jima by small boat (via Yoron and Okinoerabu Jima). and thence by aeroplane to Japan. They were to be accompanied by Okinawan students (attached to Army Headquarters as orderlies, etc.) who were to act as guides on the journey. On 19th June Major Yakumaru, Army Intelligence Officer, Major Nagano, Assistant Operations Officer, Captain Sunaga (Intelligence) and Captain Anzai (Air Corps) left the CP. On 20th June they were followed by Lt-Colonel Kimura, Air Officer, Major Miyage, Communications Officer and Captain Wasai (Intelligence), Later the same day an infiltration party of 40 men commanded by Major Matsubara made a sortie from the cave position, sustaining heavy casualties.

On 21st June at 22:00 the last message was sent to IGHQ; General Cho issued the last 32nd Army order on the same day – a general exhortation to all units to fight to the utmost. Observing that the CP was no longer tenable, Ushijima and Cho made preparations for suicide. After copious farewell toasts with the remains of the case of Black and White which the somewhat hedonistic Cho had kept with him to the last, the Commanding General, 32nd Army and his chief of staff met their death together at 04:00 on 22nd June. POW witnessed the suicides. On 23rd June Colonel Yahara, the senior staff officer (later taken prisoner) left the CP in an attempt to reach northern Okinawa and ultimately Japan on the orders of General Cho. Shortly after all the remaining personnel in the CP – about 200 – made a last attack on US positions under the command of Major Ono, chief of 32nd Army Code Section. On 24th June POW left the cave, having stayed for an extra day to care for the wounded who remained there.

POW is uncertain of the fate of the 24th and 62nd Division commanders. Lt-General Wada, commanding general 5th Artillery Command was killed at the head of his surviving troops in a suicidal assault against US forces on 21st June. The whereabouts of Maj-General Suzuki, CG 44th IMB remain in doubt; POW had heard at the Mabuni headquarters that Suzuki, accompanied by about ten soldiers, had left his command in mid-June in an effort to slip through US lines to Kunigami Gun.

32nd Army Relations with Other Echelons

As a result of the isolation of 32nd Army Headquarters and its main strength after the US landing on Okinawa, subordinate units on other islands of the Nansei Shoto formerly under the command of 32nd Army were detached and assigned to other echelons. On about 15th April control of the 28th Division and other forces in the Sakishima Gunto was transferred to the 10th Area Army (Formosan Army). The 64th IMB and attached units in the Amami Gunto were not taken from the 32nd Army's jurisdiction until late in the campaign, however; POW stated that in June they were put under the command of the Western District Army, which has been converted to a tactical command. There was never any attempt made to secure reinforcement from Tokuno Jima or any other islands of the Nansei Group, as it was recognised by 32nd Army Headquarters that the units stationed on these islands had barely enough troops to defend their assigned territories. While Army headquarters was at Mabuni, two soldiers from Amami Oshima reached there; they declared that they had been sent from Naze Oshima in company with an officer bearing a message to 32nd Army Headquarters; the officer had been killed en route and they had no idea of either the contents of the letter or the purpose of their mission.

Aside from the transmission of intelligence reports and the despatch of a few technical advisors to the 32nd Army to assist in the operation, IGHQ played a very insignificant part in the conduct of the defence of Okinawa. There was a major or lt-colonel on the staff who was charged with the duty of acting as liaison between IGHQ and the 32nd Army staff and collecting battle lessons (senji kunren) of the 32nd Army and similar information about the campaign; he exercised no influence on the conduct of the battle, however. (This officer had previously visited Okinawa from October 1944 to January 1945 for staff conferences.) In February 1945 a Major Kyoso, an artillery expert and an instructor at the Artillery Staff College was sent to 32nd Army Headquarters on temporary duty to assist in the preparation of defence plans. He gave daily lectures to groups of officers on the defence scheme of the island, stressing the artillery situation. Unfortunately for Major Kyoso, the US

Above: *'Fat Man' – a bomb of this type was detonated over Nagasaki on 9th August 1945. The bomb had a yield equivalent to approximately 20,000 tons of TNT.*

landing came somewhat prematurely for his expectations and he was unable to return, but was attached to the staff of the 44th IMB. POW believes that this officer remains at large in Kunigami Gun. In January 1945 a Major Jin was sent to 32nd Army Headquarters from Headquarters 6th Air Army to act as liaison officer between the two commands. He was ordered to return to Japan at the beginning of June with observations made by 32nd Army on the effects of the kamikaze suicide plane attacks on US targets and suggestions for their improvement. Although it had been arranged that a float plane from Tokuno was to pick him up off Mabuni for the flight to Japan, the aircraft was not forthcoming and Jin was at last forced to set out by small boat for the islands to the north on about 4th June. His efforts were apparently rewarded, as IGHQ later sent word to Okinawa that the major had safely reached Japan.

At the outset of the Okinawa operation IGHQ sent a dispatch to the 32nd Army signed by the Assistant Chief of the General Staff wishing the Army the best of luck in the coming battle and deeply regretting the fact that it was being forced to fight a large-scale action on such slender resources; POW records that the message was received with bitter amusement. Although consistent appeals for reinforcements were made by Ushijima and Cho, IGHQ' only reply was exhortations and encouraging words; no actual promises of any surface-borne reinforcements were made. According to POW, IGHQ at one time planned to return two regiments of the 9th Division to Okinawa at the beginning of 1945, but was compelled to abandon this idea because of inadequate shipping facilities. [IN: This information is completely unsubstantiated by other sources.]

32nd Army headquarters was notified by Tokyo that an airborne infiltration would be carried out on Yontan airfield on 24th May with the object of doing as much damage as possible to US aircraft and installations there; any survivors from among the infiltrators were ordered to attempt to join Japanese units in Kunigami Gun. In addition it was reported from Tokyo that the 6th Air Army was to send six battalions of airborne infantry to Okinawa by glider at the beginning of June.

From the beginning of the Okinawa campaign to the breakup of 32nd Army Headquarters on 20th June, 32nd Army battle lessons (*senji kunren*) were radioed almost daily to IGHQ by Major Yakumaru (intelligence officer) and Major Nagano (assistant operations officer). The battle lessons, a compilation of 32nd Army Headquarters and lower echelon reports on the Okinawa campaign, gave a detailed history of the action, as well as comments on tactics used by both sides and suggestions for improvements in combat techniques. The longest one sent was the account of the 3rd May counter-attack and its failure written by Colonel Yahara. POW can recall only two specific tactical recommendations made in the battle lessons: one that the standard anti-tank satchel charges be increased in weight from five kilograms to seven or eight kilograms and the other that they increase the distance between the so-called 'octopus pot' foxholes (kakutsubo) in preparing defensive positions in front of caves and similar entrenchments,

32nd Army Intelligence

Before the beginning of the Okinawa campaign, 32nd Army Headquarters had little advance information on the nature and size of the US forces about to attack the island. POW declared that a report came in March from the Harbin [NE China] *Tokumu Kikan* saying that the 1st and 6th Marine Divisions were preparing to attack Okinawa. The identity of the other divisions involved remained unknown until after the US landing. POW was familiar with Tenth Army, the 7th, 96th and 27th Divisions, but had not heard of the presence of the 77th Division, the elements of the 2nd Marine Division or either of the two corps.

Intelligence of US troop movements, order of battle information, etc. was largely secured by special teams of espionage personnel called shoko sekko tai (officer patrol units) operating behind US lines for short periods. These teams were usually composed of an officer and four or five NCOs all dressed in civilian clothes; most or all of the NCOs were Okinawans or Okinawan-speaking and the patrols usually travelled by day with groups of Okinawan civilians (many of them were in Military Government custody at various times) noting positions and troop activities. When specific information was desired by 32nd Army about an area in US held territory, it would forward the information desired to the subordinate unit most directly concerned. This unit, (generally one of the divisions or brigades) would then send several of its officer patrol units through the lines to get the information. The patrols were usually gone for a period of four to ten days, and POW asserted that the great majority of them returned safely through the lines. Despite this ease of manoeuvre, the espionage teams were not too accurate in their appraisals of US positions. They located the 96th Division CP at Futema, but erroneously thought it the Tenth Army CP. Later in the operation, they found III Amphibious Corps CP in Naha but misidentified it as the 6th Marine Division CP. Other than this, they were unable to find any US division CP; they reported to Army Headquarters that, as US divisions moved about very frequently, it was extremely difficult to locate their

CPs. In addition to this rather unimpressive information, however, POW believes that the patrols did furnish considerable intelligence on troop movements and dispositions.

There was little information obtained from captured documents, POW knew of only one, a gridded map of Okinawa which had been captured early in the operation. With the exception of two pilots captured in March, there were no American troops taken prisoner during the operation. The two airmen, according to POW, were flown directly to Japan after capture.

Oddly enough, the Japanese believed that US forces on Okinawa were using Okinawans as espionage agents behind the Japanese lines. A number of 'suspicious characters' were apprehended and questioned at Army headquarters by various amateur interrogators, including POW. Nothing was proved against them, however.

32nd Army Personalities

Generally speaking the 32nd Army staff section was distinguished among Japanese Army staffs for its progressiveness. It had been completely reorganised by Cho after he became chief of staff and included a great number of the 'bright young men' of IGHQ. As a group it operated smoothly and the intelligence and alertness of its members is in general reflected in the ability with which the defence of Okinawa was conducted.

Colonel Yahara, the senior staff officer, is a comparatively young man with wide experience and an excellent capacity for tactical direction. A cool and rational thinker, his appraisal of the Okinawan situation was from the first pessimistic and he served as an effective brake on some of the more impulsive designs of other staff members.

Lt-General Ushijima Mitsuru was a quietly-spoken competent officer with a faculty for choosing capable subordinates. He had the quality of inspiring confidence among his troops and was held in great respect by them. Early in the war he had been an infantry group commander in Burma. Prior to his assignment as Commanding General of the 32nd Army he was commandant of the Japanese Military Academy at Zama. He was to be promoted to General in August 1945.

Cho Isamu was a lt-general at the age of 51 when most of his classmates at the JMA were still colonels. He was a keen, vigorous man with an extremely aggressive personality who was feared as much as he was respected. Known in the Army and even in private circles as a strict disciplinarian requiring order and exactness in the smallest details, he did not, however, fall into the error, common to the so-called 'spit and polish' soldier, of letting an obsession with minor details injure his grasp of major issues. He was known as an extraordinarily efficient staff man and manifested this very noticeably in his conduct of the Okinawan campaign.

In the early 1930s Cho was sent to the United States as an exchange officer and spent two years there. On his return to Japan he was stationed for a considerable time at IGHQ in Tokyo until 1939, when he was ordered to China, serving there as chief of staff of the 26th Infantry Division and assistant chief of staff of the North China Expeditionary Force (North China Area Army). He was promoted to maj-general in October 1941. As the outbreak of the Greater East Asia War he became assistant chief of staff of the Southern Army and participated in the Malaya and Burma campaigns. In July 1942 he was transferred to the Military Affairs Bureau of the War Department, where he remained until receiving his appointment as chief of staff, 32nd Army.

Although believing in the creed of the Japanese military man with orthodox fervour, Cho, retained a logical outlook and a well-balanced view of the situation. He recognised that it was impossible for Japan to win the battle of Okinawa without large reinforcements. Therefore his hope in the campaign was to fight a delaying action until these reinforcements could arrive. He continued sending appeals for additional troops as late as 10th May and until that time believed that IGHQ would at least attempt to send some, for it was his firm conviction that the fall of Okinawa meant the loss of the war. There was never any question of surrendering in his mind. When the surrender message from General Buckner was received at 32nd Army Headquarters, Cho and Ushijima both laughed and declared that, as samurai, it would not be consonant with their honour to entertain such a proposal. (It should be noted that this message was received at 32nd Army about 17th June, approximately one week after it was dropped within the Japanese lines.)

When it finally became evident that resistance was at an end, Cho prepared for suicide. However, he remarked that he saw no reason for all members of the staff to do likewise and accordingly sent various staff officers to Tokyo on his own initiative, feeling that it would be senseless for them to die on Okinawa, when they could be more useful in the future both to Japan and to themselves if they remained alive. Cho was not at all pleased with the prospect of dying himself; POW believes that had the chief of staff heard of the precedent set by General Yamashita's alleged escape from the Philippines, he would have abandoned the idea of committing suicide and attempted to make his way north with the others.

Before his death Cho handed POW copies of letters which he had written to several high officials in Japan, requesting POW to deliver them if he were at all able to escape from Okinawa Although the letters were taken from POW and destroyed by the military police who captured him, he was able to recall the substance of them, which follows:

To: Dr Chiba Taneaki, Imperial Household Poetry Master

The 32nd Army under its commander has fought a good battle. Our strategy, tactics and techniques, all were used to the utmost and we fought valiantly, but it was as nothing before the material strength of the enemy. With this I shall commit suicide, bearing the responsibility for a beaten army. I beg of you the favour to tell Imperial Headquarters, after my death, of my views and of the sad manner in which I met my end.

It has become evident to me that defeat of the nation's armies is inevitable, if previous strategy is continued. Please convey my humble apologies. Thank you very much for your previous favours; I shall never forget your great kindness.

I am forwarding my opinions and the battle lessons on the Okinawa operation to IGHQ through Lt Colonel [IN: Name not known], Okinawa Operation Staff Officer [Okinawa Sakusen Shumin Sambo].

To: General Anan, Minister of War

Field Marshal Umezu, Chief of the General Staff

The Okinawa campaign has ended and I can but apologise by my death for its outcome. I pray for your success in war.

To: Hashimoto Kingoro, Head of the Imperial Youth Assistance Association
Ogawa Shumei, Head of the Strong Japan Association [Kenkokkai]
Iwata, Ainosuke, Head of the Patriotic League [Aikokusha]

[IN: The Imperial Youth Assistance Association is a national organisation embracing all Japanese youth 15 years of age and above as members; the other two groups are the strongest of Japanese patriotic organisations. Colonel Hashimoto Kingoro had ordered the sinking of the USS *Panay* in the 1937 incident, and was classed as a war criminal.]

Before material supremacy one can do nothing. With my own words I assume responsibility for the defeat. American physical resources are too much for present-day Japan; it is essential that Japan reflect on this.

I hope that my countrymen will struggle to the utmost to overcome this handicap. Many thanks for your previous favours.

Above: The war is over. General Douglas MacArthur signs as Supreme Allied Commander during formal surrender ceremonies on the USS Missouri (BB-63) in Tokyo Bay. Behind General MacArthur are Lieutenant General J. Wainwright and Lieutenant General A. E. Percival.

Okinawan Civil Officials

The governor of Okinawa Prefecture, Shimada Akira (no relation to POW) was a comparatively young man who had formerly been Chief of Police of Shanghai. Although he had taken office only recently, he had a reputation as an efficient, just administrator and was well-liked in Okinawa the high regard in which he was held was in contrast to the bad feeling which had been borne by Okinawans towards his predecessor. He had flown back to Okinawa from Formosa just one day before the initial US landing and remained with the 32nd Army in Shimajiri Gun until the end.

On 19th June US forces equipped with flamethrowers attacked the cave at Mabuni (just below the 32nd Army Headquarters cave) where the governor was living, in company with the Prefectural Chief of Police (Aral) and the Chief of the Internal Affairs Bureau (Nakasone). From that time nothing was heard of them and POW believes them dead. It is POW's opinion that the governor would have responded to an appeal to surrender at that time, had it been made.

Tokumu Kikan

[IN: As a full interrogation on this organisation lies outside the scope of this report, it is emphasised that information herein given is admittedly incomplete; it should be supplemented by exhaustive higher echelon questioning.]

POW entered the *Tokumu Kikan* in 1939 as a military civilian (*gunzoku*) agent and served in the Propaganda Section (Sendew Bu) of this organisation in North China. He stated that he had applied for this work and had been accepted as a result of the influence of Lt-General Cho, whom POW had known in Tokyo. It was because of this powerful intercessor that POW was immediately received into the *Tokumu Kikan* without having to attend the special school maintained for training the members of this organisation. However, due to this fact he was not qualified as a field agent and had the classification of a specialist in propaganda work. He served for two years in the *Tokumu Kikan* office in Peking and its branch at Taton (Daido); in July 1941 he secured a discharge on grounds, admittedly somewhat spurious, of physical disability, and returned to civilian life in Japan.

The *Tokumu Kikan* is a worldwide Japanese secret service organisation with headquarters in Tokyo and branches in almost every nation. Its duties include espionage, counter-espionage, pacification of occupied countries, surveillance of civilian populations and the dissemination of propaganda. Its sphere of operation is generally different from that of the Kempei Tai and it concerns itself for the most part with civilian rather than military affairs. Its activities are little publicised to say the least; so great is the secrecy in which it operates that few *Tokumu Kikan* personnel could identify even all the people working in their own immediate organisation.

Although a military organisation, the majority of its personnel is composed of military civilians with a status similar to that which POW enjoyed while one of the brotherhood. Many of these military civilians were among the groups of extremist young officers who engineered the assassinations of prominent moderate Japanese statesmen in the notorious 'incidents' of 15th May 1931 and 26th February 1936. Exiled for participation in these affairs, they retained a very real if unofficial connection with the Japanese Army and became active agents for the *Tokumu Kikan* in the various locations they had chosen for their places of exile.

The *Tokumu Kikan* has always been active in foreign countries; before the war it had agents at every Japanese embassy where they were responsible to the military attaché. The centres of prewar activity were the United States, USSR and Germany; according to POW there was an especially flourishing Hawaii branch. POW believed that the outbreak of the Greater East Asia War put an end to the activities of the *Tokumu Kikan* in the United States, although he thought that numerous agents remain scattered throughout the South American countries.

The largest and most efficient establishment of the *Tokumu Kikan* is in China According to POW the *Tokumu Kikan* had managed to inject itself into every section and stratum of Chinese life, including the Chungking government, which was rather carefully watched by *Tokumu Kikan* agents. Agents in the field were thoroughly trained in Chinese language, customs and conditions and in fact included hundreds of native Chinese among their number. Headquarters personnel are also competent specialists in propaganda, counter-espionage and the coordination of various intelligence activities.

In addition to the China *Tokumu Kikan*, there are large units in Japanese Manchuria (the Harbin *Tokumu Kikan* is known as an especially efficient espionage collection centre) and the occupied regions of South-east Asia. The organisation in Japan is directly under the control of the Tokyo headquarters. Activities in Manchuria are directed from headquarters of the Kwantung Army, in Malaya, Indo-China, Netherlands East Indies, etc. from the Southern Army Headquarters at Singapore, and in China from the China Expeditionary Army Headquarters and the Northern Area Army Headquarters. POW insisted that there has never been any *Tokumu Kikan* activity on Okinawa due to the docile nature of the civilian population.

POW confirmed the existence of the Navy *Tokumu Kikan* organised on the same lines and with the same purpose in mind as its Army counterpart. Although smaller than the Army organisation, it, too, apparently operates on a worldwide basis. In Japan or Japanese-held areas, *Tokumu Kikan* branches are attached to the various fleets and the headquarters of large naval shore establishments. There is a particularly large Navy *Tokumu Kikan* Branch at Amoy.

In general Army and Navy *Tokumu Kikan* operate in different assigned sectors and there is seldom much conflict between the two, except in the case of areas like Shanghai where there are large detachments of both, a condition which inevitably gives rise to the usual inter-service bickering, nowhere more prominent than among rival intelligence organisations.

According to POW there was no cooperation between the *Tokumu Kikan* and similar undercover groups of other nations. In the case of the Gestapo POW noted that, far from cooperating with that agency, Japanese authorities have caught and executed a number of Gestapo agents since the outbreak of the Greater East Asia War.

The *Tokumu Kikan* branch at Peking to which POW was attached in 1939–1941 operated under the orders of the North China Area Army and IGHQ with subsections (called *bunshitsu*) at Taton (*Daido*), Chijanshiang (*Sekkasho*), Jishang (*Joshu*) and Kaifang (*Kaifu*) and numerous smaller posts scattered throughout North China. It was commanded by a Colonel Shinoda and had a staff of over 400 at the time. It was divided into four sections each commanded by a major: Operations (*Sakusen*), Pacification (*Sembu*), Intelligence (*Joho*) and Propaganda (*Senden*). Although the four sections were theoretically on a level, in actual fact Operations and Pacification exercised a controlling power over the other two, which were primarily field agencies. Pacification and Propaganda were the two more obvious sections of the *Tokumu Kikan* and little attempt was made to conceal their identity. Operations and Intelligence, however, were scarcely known and operated in the greatest secrecy.

Operations, with a staff of about 20, concerned itself with the obtaining of tactical intelligence from civilian and other sources and was principally a planning and coordinating unit.

Intelligence, with some 3,000 personnel, including a few officers, numerous Chinese spies, informants and an assortment of odd Sax Rohmer characters [Sax Rohmer: author of the Fu Manchu mystery stories] was charged with the actual securing of intelligence information and forwarding it to headquarters;

Pacification, a group of about 10 specialists in propaganda technique, directed its efforts towards the creation of a Chinese population, friendly and holding favourable dispositions in general towards the Japanese forces.

Propaganda, with about 100 personnel including a number of Chinese, worked directly with the civilian population and for the most part was engaged in carrying out the projects conceived by Pacification, as well as promoting good will among the Chinese in a general way.

As a member of Pacification, POW's work was divided into two categories: civilian propaganda and POW propaganda. In the former connection, he wrote various propaganda leaflets for general distribution, supervised the spreading of goodwill among different civilian elements by the presentation of plays, free entertainments, etc., and the writing and dissemination of popular slogans along the lines of *Mekkyo Wahei* which can be roughly translated as 'Return to peace by killing off the Communists'. The other half of his work consisted of the indoctrination of captured Chinese POWs with an eye to their use by the Japanese. On the arrival of a group of recently captured Chinese POWs, POW would bustle out to greet them with food, entertainers, and a fairly effective propaganda line about their part in the new Japanised China. After the prisoners had been rendered favourably disposed as a result of the efforts of POW and his assistants, POW selected about half of them – the best physical and mental specimens of the group – and enrolled them in the Japanese-controlled puppet army, with an officer's commission given to the highest ranking person among them. The remaining POWs were sent to the coal mines to help dig out the foundations of the Greater East Asia Co-Prosperity Sphere. POW regarded this system as quite efficient and could recall few instances of its breaking down.

In general the propaganda line followed in China was founded on fear of Communism and the desire of building up a Sino-Japanese uniracial movement. Cultural similarities of China and Japan were stressed and Japanese propagandists like POW professed to be great admirers of the Chinese and their ways. According to POW, Japanese propaganda in North China was eminently successful, despite the admitted propensity of POWs and others like him for pursuing the local fleshpots with more ardour than the official policy of Greater East Asian Co-operation.

Defence of Japan

The coming US invasion of the Japanese home islands was a continual topic of conversation among 32nd Army staff officers both before and after the landing on Okinawa. Although there was considerable disagreement as to where an invasion would take place, the majority opinion was that the landing would be made in Honshu, probably in either Chiba, Shizuoka or Kanegawa Prefectures; General Cho believed that Chiba would be the place selected. POW pointed out at this juncture that in recent years the problems involved in a defence of Chiba and Shizuoka Prefectures against an enemy landing had received special attention at the War College and all Army staff schools. These areas have long been the traditional manoeuvring and training grounds for Japanese Army units and nowhere is the Japanese staff more familiar with the quality and potentialities of the terrain.

At the time of US landings on Okinawa 32nd Army Headquarters received a report from IGHQ that 50 new divisions were being activated in the Japanese home islands out of all remotely able-bodied men not already in the Army or the Navy. In March, prior to this broadcast, a captain (artillery), 1st lieutenant, (infantry) and other officers from the Okinawa Regimental District Headquarters were flown to 6th Depot Division Headquarters at Kumamoto to join a new division which was reportedly forming there.

In November 1944 POW visited Japan for a month and observed many signs of preparation for an invasion. He observed coast defences in Miyazaki and Oita Prefectures and elaborate systems of pillboxes, caves and other entrenchments dug in the hills just inland of the beaches, which were already being manned. However, at that time there had not yet been any order for civilians to evacuate coastal areas. He had heard that a powerful network of fortifications was being constructed in southern Kyushu and along the Pacific coasts of Shikoku and Honshu, the latter areas under the direct supervision of the Eastern District Army.

POW observed a large paratroop unit training at Takachiho in Miyazaki Prefecture, Kyushu. He estimated from the number of barracks that three regiments were stationed there. While he was in the vicinity (December 1944), they held jump practice almost every day.

Japanese surrender signatories arrive aboard the USS Missouri *(BB-63) in Tokyo Bay.*

Appendices

1 JAPANESE 32ND ARMY ORDER OF BATTLE, MARCH 1945

Army Units

Unit	Strength
Army Troops	
Headquarters	1,070
Ordnance Depot	1,498
Ordnance Duty Unit	150
Field Freight Depot	1,167
36th Signal Regiment	1,912
Okinawa Army Hospital	204
27th Field Water Purification Unit	244
Well-Digging Unit	34
Defence Construction Unit	108
7th Fortress Construction Duty Company	322
2nd Field Construction Duty Company	366
24th Infantry Division	
Headquarters	267
22nd Infantry Regiment	2,796
32nd Infantry Regiment	2,870
89th Infantry Regiment	2,809
42nd Field Artillery Regiment	2,321
24th Reconnaissance Regiment	346
24th Engineer Regiment	777
24th Transport Regiment	1,158
Signal Unit	275
Decontamination Training Unit	77
Ordnance Repair Unit	57
Veterinary Hospital	11
Water Supply and Purification Unit	241
1st Field Hospital	174
2nd Field Hospital	181

62nd Infantry Division

Unit	Strength
Headquarters	65
63rd Brigade	
Headquarters	129
11th Independent Infantry Battalion	1,091
12th Independent Infantry Battalion	1,085
13th Independent Infantry Battalion	1,058
14th Independent Infantry Battalion	1,085
273rd Independent Infantry Battalion	683
64th Brigade	
Headquarters	121
15th Independent Infantry Battalion	1,076
21st Independent Infantry Battalion	1,080
22nd Independent Infantry Battalion	1,071
23rd Independent Infantry Battalion	1,089
272nd Independent Infantry Battalion	683
Engineer Unit	255
Signal Unit	359
Transport Unit	300
Field Hospital	371
Veterinary Hospital	22
44th Independent Mixed Brigade	
Headquarters	63
2nd Infantry Regiment	2,046
15th Independent Mixed Regiment	1,885
Artillery Unit	330
Engineer Unit	161

5th Artillery Command

Unit	Strength
Headquarters	147
1st Medium Artillery Regiment	856
23rd Medium Artillery Regiment	1,143
7th Heavy Artillery Regiment	526
100th Independent Heavy Artillery Battalion	565
1st Independent Artillery Mortar Regiment	613
1st Light Mortar Battalion	633
2nd Light Mortar Battalion	615

21st Anti-aircraft Artillery Command

Headquarters	71
27th Independent Anti-aircraft Artillery Battalion	505
70th Field Anti-aircraft Artillery Battalion	513
80th Field Anti-aircraft Artillery Battalion	517
81st Field Anti-aircraft Artillery Battalion	514
103rd Independent Machine-Cannon Battalion	336
104th Independent Machine-Cannon Battalion	338
105th Independent Machine-Cannon Battalion	337

Machine-Gun Units

3rd Independent Machine-Gun Battalion	340
4th Independent Machine-Gun Battalion	344
14th Independent Machine-Gun Battalion	334
17th Independent Machine-Gun Battalion	331

Anti-tank Units

3rd Independent Anti-tank Battalion	363
7th Independent Anti-tank Battalion	353
22nd Independent Anti-tank Battalion	402
32nd Independent Anti-tank Company	144

11th Shipping Group

Headquarters	100
7th Shipping Engineer Branch Depot	600
23rd Shipping Engineer Regiment	850
26th Shipping Engineer Regiment	550
5th Sea Raiding Base Headquarters	42
1st Sea Raiding Squadron	104
2nd Sea Raiding Squadron	104
3rd Sea Raiding Squadron	104
26th Sea Raiding Squadron	104
27th Sea Raiding Squadron	104
28th Sea Raiding Squadron	104
29th Sea Raiding Squadron	104
1st Sea Raiding Base Battalion	886

Unit	Strength
2nd Sea Raiding Base Battalion	874
3rd Sea Raiding Base Battalion	877
26th Sea Raiding Base Battalion	908
27th Sea Raiding Base Battalion	897
28th Sea Raiding Base Battalion	900
29th Sea Raiding Base Battalion	900

49th Line of Communication Sector

Headquarters	202
72nd Land Duty Company	508
83rd Land Duty Company	496
103rd Sea Duty Company	711
104th Sea Duty Company	724
215th Independent Motor Transport Company	181
259th Independent Motor Transport Company	182

Engineer Units

66th Independent Engineer Battalion	865
14th Field Well Drilling Company	110
20th Field Well Drilling Company	110

19th Air Sector Command

Headquarters	41
29th Field Airfield Construction Battalion	750
44th Airfield Battalion	377
50th Airfield Battalion	360
56th Airfield Battalion	380
3rd Independent Maintenance Unit	120
Makoto 1st Maintenance Company	90
118th Independent Maintenance Unit	100
6th Fortress Construction Duty Company	330
Detachment, 20th Air Regiment	27
10th Field Meteorological Unit	80
26th Air-Ground Radio Unit	117
46th Independent Air Company	132
1st Branch Depot, 5th Field Air Repair Depot	130
21st Air Signal Unit	310
Okinawa Branch, Army Air Route Department	359
223rd Specially Established Garrison Company	200
224th Specially Established Garrison Company	200
225th Specially Established Garrison Company	200

27th Tank Regiment   750

Army total	*66,636* [1]

Japanese Navy Units

Unit	Strength
Okinawa Base Force	3,400
(Headquarters, Coast Defence, and Anti-aircraft Personnel)	
27th Motor Torpedo Boat Squadron	200
33rd Midget Submarine Unit	130
37th Torpedo Maintenance Unit	140
Torpedo Working Unit	130
81mm Mortar Battery	150
Oroku Transmitting Station	30
Naha Branch, Sasebo Naval Stores Department	136
Naha Branch, Sasebo Transportation Department	136
Naha Navy Yard, Sasebo Naval Base	53
Oroku Detachment, 951st Air Group	600
Nansei Shoto Air Group	2,000
226th Construction Unit	1,420
3210th Construction Unit	300
Navy total	8,825 [2]

Okinawan Personnel

Unit	Strength
502nd Special Guard Engineer Unit	900
503rd Special Guard Engineer Unit	700
504th Special Guard Engineer Unit	700
Blood-and-Iron-for-the-Emperor Duty Unit	750
Boeitai assigned to the Army	16,600
Boeitai assigned to the Navy	1,100
Students	600
Regular conscripts not included under Army units	2,000

Okinawan total   23,350

Total Japanese Strength on Okinawa   c. 100,000 [3]

Notes

1. This figure represents the total Japanese Army strength. Included in it, however, are an estimated 5,000 Okinawans, mostly regular conscripts, who were integrated into Japanese units.
2. This total represents both regular naval ratings and the Japanese, Korean, and Okinawan military civilians who were employed in the naval land combat organisation.
3. Strength figures have been rounded.

Source: Charles S. Nichols and Henry I. Shaw, Okinawa: Victory in the Pacific, Historical Branch, G-3 Division, US Marine Corps, Washington, DC, 1955, pp. 302–4.

2 TABLES OF ORGANISATION

32nd Army

Staff

Commander	Lt-General Ushijima Mitsuru
Chief of Staff	Lt-General Cho Isamu
Operations Officer	Colonel Yahara Hiromichi
Staff Officers	
	Lt-Colonel Kimura Masaharu
	Major Jin Naominichi – Aviation
	Major Miyake Tadeo
	Major Kusumaru Kanenori
	Major Nagano Hideo
	Lt-Colonel Kuzuno Ryuichi
Branch Officers	
Weapons	Colonel Sakurai Mitsugi
Administration	Colonel Sato Miyoharu
Medical	Colonel Shinoda Shigeyoshi
Veterinary	Colonel Sato Takehisa
Legal Affairs	Major Wada Kazuyoshi

24th Infantry Division

Division Headquarters

Operations Section

Administrative Section

22nd Infantry Regiment

3 infantry battalions (each battalion composed of 3 infantry companies, 1 machine-gun company, 1 anti-tank company, 1 gun company[1]

Regimental gun company (2 gun platoons, 1 ammo platoon)

Signal company (2 platoons)

32nd Infantry Regiment

3 infantry battalions (each battalion 3 infantry companies, 1 machine-gun company, 1 anti-tank company, 1 gun company)

Regimental gun company (2 gun platoons, 1 ammunition platoon)

Signal company (2 platoons)

89th Infantry Regiment

3 infantry battalions (each battalion 3 infantry companies, 1 machine-gun company, 1 anti-tank company, 1 gun company)

Regimental gun company (2 gun platoons, 1 ammunition platoon)

Signal company (2 platoons)

42nd Artillery Regiment

3 artillery battalions[2]

24th Engineer Regiment

3 companies

24th Reconnaissance Regiment

3 infantry companies, 1 machine-gun company, 1 signal company

Signals Unit

2 line platoons, 1 radio platoon, 1 equipment platoon

24th Transport Regiment

3 motor companies, 2 horse companies

Other units

Ordnance Unit, Medical Unit,[4] Water Supply Unit, Veterinary Unit

62nd Infantry Division

Division Headquarters

Operations Section, Administrative Section

63rd Infantry Brigade

11th, 12th, 13th, 14th and 273rd Independent Infantry Battalions (each battalion 5 infantry companies, 1 machine-gun company, 1 infantry gun company)

64th Infantry Brigade

15th, 21st, 22nd, 23rd, and 272nd Independent Infantry Battalions (each battalion 3 infantry companies, 1 machine-gun company, 1 gun platoon)

Other units

Engineer Unit, Signals Unit, Transport Unit, Medical Unit,[4] Veterinary Unit

44th Independent Mixed Brigade

Brigade Headquarters

2nd Infantry Regiment[3]

1st, 2nd, 3rd Infantry Battalions (each battalion 3 infantry companies, 1 machine-gun company, 1 gun platoon)

Other units

Regiment gun company
Regiment anti-tank company

15th Independent Mixed Regiment

1st, 2nd, 3rd Infantry Battalions (each battalion 3 infantry companies, machine-gun company, gun platoon)
Other units
Regiment gun company
Regiment anti-tank company
Artillery Unit (2 batteries)
Signals Unit

Notes

1. 3rd bn of each regt, gun company equipped with mortars
2. 1st and 2nd Artillery Battalions had 1 x 75mm gun battery, 2 x 100mm howitzer battery and 1 supply company. 3rd Artillery Battalion had 3 x 150mm howitzer battery, 1 supply company
3. IJA medical services were extensive, including those with the unit, field hospitals and water purification personnel. The IJA kept its casualties as far forward as possible in order to speed their return to their fighting units. In addition a high proportion of the medical personnel were equipped with weapons and were expected to take part in the fighting. The typical medical unit organisation included 3 collecting companies and would be supported by a supply company and a number of field hospitals. The medical services were far less extensive in the 62nd Division and the 44th Independent Mixed Brigade than the 'Heavy' 24th Division.
4. 1st and 2nd Infantry Battalions, Regiment gun company and Regiment anti-tank company – Kunigami detachment units

3 STRENGTHS, MARCH 1945

24th Infantry Division

Division Headquarters	267
22nd Infantry Regiment	2,796
32nd Infantry Regiment	2,796
89th Infantry Regiment	2,796

42nd Artillery Regiment

Headquarters	150
1st Battalion	660
2nd Battalion	660
3rd Battalion	760

24th Reconnaissance Regiment	346
24th Engineer Regiment	777
24th Transport Regiment	1,158

Other units

Medical Battalion	355
Veterinary unit	11
Water supply company	241
Decontamination unit	77
Ordnance company	57

62nd Infantry Division

| Headquarters | 65 |

63rd Infantry Brigade

Headquarters	129
11th, 12th, 13th, 14th Independent Inf. Bns [1]	1,091 each
273rd Independent Infantry Battalion [2]	683

64th Infantry Brigade

Headquarters	129
15th, 21st, 22nd, 23rd Independent Inf. Battalions [1]	1,091 each
272nd Independent Infantry Battalion [2]	683

Other units

Engineer Unit	255
Signals Unit	359
Field Hospital	371
Veterinary Unit	22
Transport Unit	300

44th Independent Mixed Brigade

| Headquarters | 63 |

2nd Infantry Regiment

1st Battalion [3 & 4]	700
2nd Battalion [3 & 4]	700
3rd Battalion [4]	700
Regiment gun company [3]	140
Regiment anti-tank gun company [3]	140

15th Independent Mixed Regiment

Headquarters	120
3 battalions	698 each
Regiment gun company	140
Regiment anti-tank gun company	140

Notes

1. These battalions had 5 rifle companies, 1 machine-gun company, 1 infantry gun company
2. These battalions had 3 rifle companies, 1 machine-gun company, 1 gun company
3. Kunigami detachment units
4. Each battalion had 3 rifle companies, 1 machine-gun company, 1 gun company

4 US BATTLE CASUALTIES

Average weekly battle casualties of American combat divisions on Okinawa for first two weeks of full engagement and for all subsequent weeks of full engagement.

Unit	Av Weekly Battle Casualties		
	First 14 days	Subsequent	Ratio of A to B
7th Inf Div	695a	558b	1:24
27th Inf Div	1,298c	–d	–
77th Inf Div	905e	631f	1.43
96th Inf Div	1,074g	575h	1.87
1st Marine Div	1,595i	679j	2.35
6th Marine Div	1,220k	880l	1.39

Notes

a. Figures for 9th–21st April.
b. Figures for 22nd April – 23rd June, but excluding figures for 6th–26th May because the weekly numbers were affected by 7th Infantry Division's withdrawal from the line for rest on 10th–22nd May.
c. Figures for 15th–28th April.
d. After suffering exceptionally high casualties in the late April offensives, the 27th Infantry Division was permanently withdrawn from the line on 1st May for mop-up and garrison duty in the north.
e. Figures for 29th April – 12th May.
f. Figures for 13th May – 2nd June.
g. Figures for 9th–21st April.
h. Figures for 22nd April – 23rd June, but excluding figures for 29th April – 12th May because the weekly numbers were affected by the 96th Infantry Division's withdrawal from the line for rest on 30th April – 10th May.
i. Figures for 29th April – 12th May.
j. Figures for 13th May – 23rd June.
k. Figures for 6th–19th May.
l. Figures for 20th May – 23rd June.

Selected Sources and Further Reading

Books

Appleman, Roy E., *et al.*, *Okinawa: The Last Battle*, Historical Division, Department of the Army, 1971.

Belote, James, and Belote, William, *Typhoon of Steel: The Battle for Okinawa*, Harper and Row, 1970.

Boei Kenkyujo Senshishitsu (ed.), *Okinawa Homen Rikugun Sakusen, Senshi Sosho* [Okinawa Area Infantry Strategy, War History Series], Asakumo Shimbunsha, 1968.

Bradley, John H., *The Second World War: Asia and the Pacific*, West Point Military History Series, Avery Publishing, Wayne, NJ, 1984.

Buell, T. B., *Master of Sea Power*, Little Brown, 1980.

Buell, T. B., *Quiet Warrior*, Little Brown, 1974.

Coox, Alvin D., *Nomonhan: Japan against Russia, 1939*. Stanford University Press, 1985.

Dod, Karl C., *The Technical Services; The Corps of Engineers: The War against Japan*, Washington, DC: The Government Printing Office, 1966.

Fairbank, Leigh C., Jr., 'Division Engineers: Part IV Ryukus Islands (continued)', *Military Engineer*, 39, July 1947, pp. 294–99.

Frank, R.B., *Downfall*, Random House, 1999.

Inagaki, Takeshi, *Okinawa: Higu no Sakusen* [Okinawa: a strategy of tragedy], Shinchosha, 1984.

Isely, Jeter A., and Crowl, Philip A., *The US Marines and Amphibious War: Its Theory and Practice in the Pacific*, Princeton University Press, 1951.

Leed, Eric J., *No Man's Land: Combat and Identity In World War II*, Cambridge University Press, 1979.

Mikami, Masahiro, '62d Division Crisis and Commitment of the Bulk of 32 Army in the Northern Front', in *Okinawa Campaign, Data for MHX-85*, translated by Yanase Tokui, JGSDF Staff College, Tokyo, Dec 1985.

Morison, S., *History of United States Naval Operations in World War II*, Little Brown 1954–60.

Potter, E.B., *Nimitz*, Naval Institute Press, 1976.

Nichols, Charles, and Shaw, Henry I., *Okinawa: Victory in the Pacific*, Historical Branch, G-3 Division, US Marine Corps, 1955.

Nishimura, Hitoshi, 'Command and Staff Activities in the Offensive Operations on 4th May 1945', in *Okinawa Campaign, Data for MHX-85*, translated by Yanase Tokui, JGSDF Staff College, Tokyo, December 1985.

Reynolds, C.G., *The Fast Carriers*, McGraw-Hill, 1968.

Rikusen-shi kenkyu fukyu kai, (ed.), [Land Warfare Research and Publicisation Association], *Okinawa Sakusen, Dainiji Sekai Taisen Shi, Rikusenshishu* [Okinawa Strategy, History of World War II, Land Warfare History Collection], vol. 9, Hara shobo, Tokyo, 1974.

Yahara, Hiromichi, *Okinawa Kessen* [Battle of Okinawa], Yomiuri Shimbunsha, 1972.

Government Documents

US Army, 10th Army, G-1 Section; 'G-1 Periodic Reports, Numbers 1 to 14'; Okinawa, 1st April 1945 – 7th July 1945.

US Army, 10th Army, G-2 Section; 'G-2 Weekly Summary, Number 2'; Okinawa, 4th June 1945.

US Army; 'Intelligence Monograph Ryukus Campaign'; Okinawa, 1945.

US Army Forces Far East, Military History Section, ed.; 'Japanese Monograph no. 135'; *Okinawa Operations Record*, 1949.

US Army Forces, Pacific Ocean Areas, Assistant Chief of Staff, G-2 Section; 'Test of Japanese Demolitions, Technical Intelligence Bulletin No. 16'; Guam, June 1945.

US Army Ground Forces, G-2 Section; 'Information on Japanese Defensive Installations and Tactics'; 1945.

US Army, 77th Infantry Division, G-2 Section; 'G-2 Periodic Report [Daily]' Okinawa, 25th May 1945.

US Army; 'G-2 Summary – Okinawa from 27 April 1945 to 10th June 1945'; Okinawa, June 1945.

US Commander in Chief, Pacific, and Commander in Chief, Pacific Ocean Areas; 'Searching Caves: A Summary of Techniques Developed at Okinawa, CINCPAC-CINCPOA Bulletin No. 189-45'; Guam, August 1945.

US Marine Corps, 6th Marine Division; 'Sixth Marine Division on Okinawa Shima, G-2 Summary'; Okinawa, August 1945.

US War Department, Military Intelligence Division; 'Japanese tank and Antitank Warfare'; 1945.

US War Department; *TM-E 30 – 480. Handbook on Japanese Military Forces*; October 1944.

Index

Ma-Gen Fred C. Wallace, (left foreground) CG of Okinawa, reads the inscription on the memorial tablet erected in a US Marine cemetery on the island. The inscription reads, 'Died for God and Country – an American.'